The New Testament And Its Message

A   B r i e f   S u r v e y

Stanford E. Murrell

Ichthus Publications · Apollo, Pennsylvania

Copyright © 2019 by Stanford E. Murrell

This book was previously published by Chapel Library under the title *The New Covenant In Christ: A Survey of the New Testament.*

The publisher gratefully acknowledges the work of Mr. Dan Johnson, teacher of New Testament at The Evangelical Institute of Greenville, SC, whose course notes have been used by permission for some of the overview charts and book outlines.

All rights reserved. No part of this publication may be reproduced, stored in a retrieval system, or transmitted, in any form or by any means, electronic, mechanical, photocopying, recording or otherwise, without prior permission of the publisher or the Copyright Licensing Agency.

Our goal is to provide high-quality, thought-provoking books that foster encouragement and spiritual growth. For more information regarding Ichthus Publications, other IP books, or bulk purchases, visit us online or write to support@ichthuspublications.com.

Unless otherwise indicated, all Scripture quotations are taken from the King James Version.

Printed in the United States of America

The New Testament and Its Message: A Brief Survey
ISBN: 978-1-946971-47-0

www.ichthuspublications.com

*"Study to show thyself approved unto God,
a workman that needeth not to be ashamed,
rightly dividing the Word of truth."*

—2 TIMOTHY 2:15

Contents

1	In the Fullness of Time	11
2	The Conception of Christianity	33
3	Behold the Lamb!	41
4	Matthew: The King of His Kingdom	49
5	Mark: The Servant of All	61
6	Luke: The Perfect Man	75
7	John: The Son of God	87
8	Acts: Witness to the World	99
9	Romans: Faith Alone	113
10	1 Corinthians: The Cross for the Church	119
11	2 Corinthians: Ministry in the Church	127
12	Galatians: Life in Liberty	133
13	Ephesians: Union with Christ	139
14	Philippians: Joy in Unity	143
15	Colossians: Complete in Christ	151
16	1 Thessalonians: The Second Coming	155
17	2 Thessalonians: Judgment to Come	159
18	1 Timothy: Protect the Gospel	161
19	2 Timothy: Preach the Gospel	165
20	Titus: Teach the Gospel	169
21	Philemon: Grace in Practice	173
22	Hebrews: Drawing Near	177
23	James: Faith Proven by Works	185
24	1 Peter: Partaking of Christ's Sufferings	191
25	2 Peter: Knowledge of Our Lord	195

26	1 John: Fellowship with Christ	199
27	2 John: Walking in Truth	203
28	3 John: Hospitality	207
29	Jude: Keep from Falling	211
30	Revelation: Christ is Lord!	217

Appendix 1: Thirty-five Miracles of the Master   233
Appendix 2: Guidelines for Reading the Bible   235

G O D,

*who at sundry times and in divers manners
spake in time past unto the fathers by the prophets,
hath in these last days spoken unto us by*

H I S   S O N,

*whom He hath appointed Heir of all things,
by whom also He made the worlds;
who being the brightness of His Glory,
and the express image of His Person,
and upholding all things
by the Word of His Power,
when He had by Himself purged our sins,
sat down on the right hand of the*

M A J E S T Y   O N   H I G H.

— H E B R E W S   1 : 1 - 3

1

In the Fullness of Time

"But when the fullness of the time was come, God sent forth His Son, made of a woman, made under the law."

—Galatians 4:4

Prophecy Fulfilled

It is often said that with the close of the Old Testament canon of Scripture, a prolonged silence of Divine revelation ensued. This is far from being the case. Though Malachi (c. 400 B.C.) was the last physical prophetic voice to be heard, God prepared the world to receive His Son by fulfilling His promises as proclaimed by other prophets. That God's Son would someday arrive was certain, for a Divine calendar of the coming Prince had already been given to Daniel. Specifically, Israel had been promised that a command would be issued to rebuild the Holy Temple of Jerusalem. Four hundred and ninety years later, Messiah would appear (Dan. 9:24–27). The people were not to become discouraged. They were to watch and wait upon the Lord.

In the interval of time, many things happened. While the people of the covenant dreamed of their coming Deliverer, important events transpired. One of the most significant was the one which took place in Alexandria, Egypt. According to tradition, at the request of Ptolomy Philadelphus (285–247 B.C.) a group of seventy scholars translated the

Hebrew Old Testament books into the Greek language, called the *Septuagint* (meaning *seventy*). Because Greek had become the international language of the time, this remarkable translation allowed those in the Graeco-Roman world to hear and read the Scripture in their own common language. Later, the New Testament would be written originally in Greek. Many of its quotations of the Old Testament would come from the *Septuagint*, also known as the "LXX" (70). The oldest known copy of the *Septuagint* is written on vellum (antelope skin). It dates from the 5th century A.D. and is called the *Codex Alexandrinus*.

The Power of the Persians

In the *Septuagint*, the Romans could read of the prophecies predicting their own rise to power, and their destruction (Dan. 2:40–45; 7:7–14). They were merely another people on the world stage of history. Other great empires had preceded them, including the Persians. During the days of Malachi, the Persian Empire ruled the Middle East. Palestine was considered to be just a tiny province (satrapy) under the dominion of a Persian governor (satrap). The Jews enjoyed a measure of peace under their Persian masters and even prospered—always keeping in mind that the Persian Empire was destined to fall according to prophecy (Dan. 2:31–33). However, before its certain demise, the story of several mighty sovereigns would be told. The history of the Persian Empire is embodied in the deeds of powerful men:

Xerxes II	424–423 B.C.
Darius II	423–404 B.C.
Artaxerxes II	404–358 B.C.
Artaxerxes III	358–338 B.C.
Arses	338–336 B.C.
Darius III	336–331 B.C.

The Macedonian Empire

According to biblical prophecy, the Persian Empire was to be conquered by the Greeks (Dan. 2:39; 7:5–6). The rise of Philip II (382–336 B.C.), King of Macedon (359–336 B.C.) made this possible. Philip used his military and diplomatic skills to create a powerful united state at home prior to making himself ruler of an independent Greece. He became the master of Greece by winning a decisive victory at the Battle of Chaeronea (338 B.C.). The power of the Greek city-states was broken. While planning the conquest of Persia, Philip was assassinated in 336 B.C.

Taking over his father's army, Alexander (356–323 B.C.) prepared to win more of the world. Of particular interest was the conquest of Persia, which he completed in three decisive battles: Granicus (334 B.C.), Issus (333 B.C.), and Gaugamela (332 B.C.). Turning towards Egypt, Alexander marched south towards Jerusalem. The Jewish people posed no real threat. He marched into Syria taking Palestine, Tyre (331 B.C.), and Gaza with ease. Because the Jews of Jerusalem eagerly submitted to his rule, they were treated well. In fact, when Alexander drew near the city, Jewish leaders met him with a scroll of Daniel the prophet to show that he was the fulfillment of Divine prophecy (cp. Dan. 8:18–21). There would be no resistance to his rule.

Alexander continued to march south in order to conquer Egypt (332 B.C.), and established Alexandria. In 327 B.C., Alexander reached the Punjab in India. He wanted to move on to the Ganges, but his troops revolted and forced his return to Babylon. He died there in 323 B.C. at the young age of 33, having cried his famous lament "I have no more worlds to conquer!"

Palestine under the Ptolemies

Having no heir, Alexander left behind two things. First, he left behind a world in which he had disseminated Greek language, culture, and philosophy. Later it would be said "while Rome conquered Greece, Greece conquered Rome." The concept is that while the Romans won the military victory, Greek thought and culture dominated and transformed all of Roman society. Then second, Alexander left behind a fragmented empire. His generals struggled for power before dividing the empire into four spheres of influence, the two most important being the Ptolemies in Egypt and Palestine, and the Seleucids in Persia.

Ptolemy I Soter (d. 283 B.C.) became the ruler of Egypt (305–285 B.C.). Palestine came under his sphere of influence. Ptolemy occupied the first part of his reign in defending himself from outside attacks and consolidating his government. Because of his graciousness to the Jews, many of them settled in Alexandria, Egypt, a city renowned for its economic and cultural advancements.

Ptolemy II Philadelphus (c. 308–246 B.C.) was the son and successor of Ptolemy I Soter. Under his reign (285–246 B.C.), Egypt reached its greatest height. After success in foreign wars, Ptolemy II enlarged the Museum and Library in Alexandria and invited many leading Greek intellectuals to his court.

Ptolemy III Euergetes (d. 222 B.C.) was the son and successor of Ptolemy II. As king (246–222 B.C.), he subdued Syria and Cilicia and returned to Egypt with a tremendous amount of wealth.

Ptolemy IV Philopator (d. 205 B.C.) was the son and successor of Ptolemy III. He began his reign by killing his mother, Berenice. The decline of the Ptolemies' power is attributed to his indolent reign (221–205 B.C.).

Ptolemy V Epiphanes (d. 181 B.C.) succeeded his father, Ptolemy IV, while still a child. It was during his reign (205–181 B.C.) that court intrigues and conflicts arose which were to overshadow the dynasty for the remainder of the Ptolemaic Period. Despite the treachery of the times, Epiphanes survived and recorded several things associated with his reign. In 1799 a black basalt stone was found called the Rosetta Stone. Recorded in Greek, hieroglyphic (a form of ancient writing, mainly in pictorial characters), and demotic (a simplified form of the ancient Egyptian writing) was the coronation ceremony held in 196 BC for Ptolemy V. In addition, information was detailed on the steps taken to secure the loyalty of the priesthood. The inscriptions on the Rosetta Stone became the key to understanding other inscriptions of the ancient world of Egypt.

Ptolemy VI Philometer (d. 145 B.C.) ruled Egypt from 180–145 B.C. He was the successor to his father, Ptolemy V. Forced to share royal power with his brother, Philometer helped bring about the first intervention of Rome in Egyptian affairs.

Ptolemy VIII Physcon (d. 116 B.C.) ruled Egypt from 145–116 B.C. Usurping the throne from his brother, Physcon ruled with great cruelty and so provoked revolts. He drove the scholars from Alexandria.

Ptolemy IX Lathyrus (d. 81 B.C.) was king of Egypt from 116–81 B.C. He was the successor to his father Physcon. Lathyrus was driven from the throne in 107 BC but returned in 88 B.C. after expelling his brother Ptolemy X Alexander, whose co-rule his mother had compelled him to accept.

Ptolemy X Alexander (d. 88 B.C.) was king of Egypt from 107–88. With the help of his mother, he supplanted his brother, Ptolemy IX, until the latter was finally defeated in a civil war. In 88 B.C., Lathyrus won back the throne in another civil war.

Ptolemy XI (d. 80 B.C.). When Lathyrus died, his successor married his widow only to murder her and in turn be murdered by a mob.

Ptolemy XII (d. 51 B.C.), the illegitimate son of Ptolemy IX, ruled Egypt from 80–51 B.C. His mismanagement of the affairs of state brought about his expulsion. He was restored to the throne only by the power of the armies of Rome.

Ptolemy XIV (d. 44 B.C.) was the last Macedonian king of Egypt (47–44 B.C.). By the order of Julius Caesar he married his sister Cleopatra VII, who ruled with him. Cleopatra arranged his murder so that her own son by Caesar could take the throne.

Ptolemy XV, the son of Cleopatra and Caesar, did become king and ruled Egypt from 44-30 B.C. After Cleopatra's suicide (30 B.C.), he was killed by Octavian. Following his death, Egypt became a Roman province.

The Seleucid Rulers

Constantly contesting the Ptolemaic line for control of Palestine were the Seleucids. This Greek dynasty descended from Seleucus, another general of Alexander the Great, who initially took the Persian part of the divided empire. The Seleucids ruled over a vast dominion stretching from Asia Minor to northwest India. However, by the time Rome suppressed them in 63 B.C., all that was left to them was Syria. Until that happened, the kings of Syria enjoyed ruling over great spheres of influence. Their major rulers are:

Seleucus I	312–280 B.C.
Antiochus I	280–262 B.C.
Antiochus II	261–246 B.C.
Seleucus II	246–226 B.C.
Seleucus III	226–223 B.C.
Antiochus III	223–187 B.C.
Seleucus IV	187–175 B.C.
Antiochus IV Epiphanes	175–163 B.C.
Antiochus V	163–162 B.C.
Demetrius I	162–150 B.C.

Demetrius II and Alexander Balas contend for the throne

Alexander Balas	150–145 B.C.
Demetrius II	145–139 B.C.

He honored Simon as high priest c.143 B.C.

Antiochus VII	139–134 B.C.

The death of Antiochus VII brought to an end Seleucid power over Palestine. In 198 B.C., Antiochus III the Great expelled the Egyptians from Palestine and annexed it to the Seleucid Empire. Severe suffering came to the Jews when Antiochus IV decided to enforce the Hellenistic or Greek culture upon the nation. Between 167–165 B.C., he sacked Jerusalem and desecrated the Holy Temple by offering a sow on its altar. He constructed an altar to Jupiter and presented sacrifices to the Olympian god Zeus on the altar of burnt offering. He threatened death for anyone who performed the covenant ritual of circumcision and sold thousands of Jewish families into slavery. All copies of the sacred Scriptures were destroyed. Anyone discovered with a portion of the Bible was tortured. The abominable actions of Antiochus ignited the patriotic Maccabean family to lead a heroic revolt, guided first by the aged priest Mattathias (c. 168 B.C.) and then by his five sons: Judas (166–160 B.C.), Jonathan (160–142 B.C.), Simon (142–134 B.C.), John (d. 161 B.C.), and Eleazar (d. 163 B.C.).

The Maccabees

As a leading Jewish family, the Maccabees, also known as the Hasmoneans, were able to initially resist the influences of Greek culture on Israel and its religion during the Syrian rule over Palestine. When Mattathias died (166 B.C.), leadership fell upon Judas Maccabeus (Ben Mattathias). A warrior of great military skill, Judas included in his arsenal of revolt the use of guerrilla warfare. His extraordinary victories against overwhelming circumstances resulted in defeat after defeat of the Syrian armies and a cleansing of the Temple (165 B.C.), which instituted the Feast of Dedication. In the years that followed, Judas united the offices of priest and civil authority in himself. By the force of his personality he brought peace to the area and freedom to the nation. Palestine would enjoy a 100 year period of semi-independence from Syrian control. The subsequent Hasmonaean priest-rulers which governed included the brothers of Judas: Jonathan (160–142 B.C.) and Simon (142–134 B.C.).

John Hyrcanus (134–105 B.C.), the son of Simon, was able to carry on the political and religious work of his father. He enjoyed victories in the Trans-Jordan region, in Samaria (where he destroyed the rival

Temple on Mt. Gerizim), and in Edom. During his time, two great parties arose in Judaism, the Pharisees and the Sadducees. The monastic sect called Essenes also appeared according to Philo, Josephus, Pliny and the Dead Sea Scrolls. The Khirbet Qumran served as the central location of the Essenes on the northwest shores of the Dead Sea. It was founded c. 110 B.C. and continued until about 37 A.D.

Subsequent rulers to John Hyrcanus did not serve the nation of Israel well. For example, Aristobulus I (d. 104 B.C.) and his sons brought disgrace to the Maccabean name during the years 105–67 B.C. The nation was weakened politically until finally, in the year 63 B.C., Palestine was conquered by the Romans under the great general Pompeii. Antipater, an Idumean or descendant of Esau, was appointed ruler of Judea. He in turn was succeeded by his son Herod (the Great), who was appointed king of Judea in 37 B.C. and ruled until 4 B.C.

Alexander Jannaeus (103–76 B.C.) was a determined conqueror who secured the destiny of the Hasmonaean dynasty by alienating the Pharisees. Many of the Dead Sea Scrolls date from this period and later (c. 1 B.C. to A.D. 70). His wife, Alexandra, emerged to exercise control in political affairs (76–67 B.C.). Her elder son, Hyrcanus II (d. 30 B.C.), was appointed high priest. At her death, Antipater (the governor of Idumeae) persuaded Hyrcanus to go to Petra and enlist the assistance of the Nabatean prince Aretas, in order to win the people of Judea for him against the claims of his brother Aristobulus. When the struggle could not be resolved, an appeal was made to Rome which sided with the Hasmonaean monarchy. Aristobulus II (66–63 B.C.) was carried to Rome and put on public display as part of Pompeii's triumph. Pompeii did more than settle a political dispute. He brought Palestine under Roman control by organizing the Decapolis (lit. *ten cities*) league in Trans-Jordan to balance the power of Judea, which was reduced in size.

The Rise of Rome to Rule the World

All of this took place against the background of the rise of Rome to world conquest, which began as early as 753 B.C. Romans pretended to believe that their city was founded by Romulus who, according to legend, was cared for with his twin, Remus, by a 'foster-mother' wolf. The significance of this myth is that it acknowledged a debt to a past that was associated with the mysterious people called Etruscans, who held a special place of honor for the wolf (cp. Rom. 1:18–23). Gifted in the use of metallurgy, the Etruscans wielded iron weapons as they went forth to conquer.

Near the end of the sixth century B.C., Rome broke away from the influence of the Etruscans during a period of general unrest on the Italian peninsula. Anxious to assert themselves, the warriors of the small community on the south bank of the Tiber River in Italy went forth to conquer. In the years and centuries to come, military success was not stopped until all rivals had been subdued.

The greatest resistance to this new Roman domination proved to be Carthage, whose ships dominated the commerce of the Mediterranean. The protracted Punic Wars ensued in which the whole western Mediterranean was at stake. The First Punic War (264–241 B.C.) resulted in Rome's acquisition of Sicily. The Second Punic War (218–202 B.C.) forced Carthage to become a dependent entity paying tribute. Prior to being defeated, the Carthaginian general Hannibal made his great march across the Alps with an army which included elephants, and defeated a Roman force twice his size at Lake Trasimene and Cannae (217 and 216 B.C.). Tragically, at the last, Hannibal met his defeat at Zama in 202 B.C. and the war ended. The Third Punic War (149–146 B.C.) came to an end when the Roman general Scipio [Aemilianus] captured the city of Carthage and destroyed it completely, thereby firmly establishing the dominion of Rome over Spain and North Africa.

At the same time, Macedonia was made a Roman province, as was the territory of Achaia (146 B.C.). In 133 B.C., at the death of Attalus III, the king of Pergamum, he graciously willed his domain to the Romans. From this bequeathment came the province of Asia. Meanwhile, fighting continued in the eastern part of Asia Minor until Pompeii was able to subdue Pontus and Caucasus. In 63 B.C., the great general made Syria a province and then went on to annex Judea. In Gaul, from 58 to 57 B.C., Julius Caesar fought until that area also was made into a Roman province.

Finally, the appetite of Rome was satiated. For 500 years, Roman soldiers had routed every force they faced in a terrifying manner. The army was organized in legions of 5,000 which attacked in solid phalanxes with long spike spears. When hand to hand combat was necessary, the soldiers were well trained to fight in close quarters to the death while showing no mercy. And so it was, from an obscure village, Rome had risen to rule the world.

Roman Rulers in New Testament Times

The expeditious territorial expansion produced significant changes in the life of the Roman people. A strong ruler was essential if the vast and diverse empire was to be held together. Julius Caesar was such a leader.

Pompeii, Caesar, and Crassus had formed the First Triumvirate (60 B.C.). This was followed by Caesar's Gallic Wars (58–51 B.C.) and then by civil war as Caesar fought for control of the empire from Pompeii. In the end, Caesar was assassinated in March of 44 B.C.

The death of Caesar led to the forming of the Second Triumvirate consisting of Mark Antony, Octavian, and Lepidus in 43 B.C. When peace among these ambitious men broke down, civil war emerged. The battles at Philippi (42 B.C.) and Actium (31 B.C.), left Octavian, the young grand-nephew of Caesar, as the new and only Roman emperor. Changing his name to Augustus, he ruled Rome from 27 B.C. to A.D. 14.

While the leading figures of Rome fought for control of the empire, Palestine itself was ruled by Antipater the Idumaean under a Roman grant (55–43 B.C.). He was assisted by his sons, Herod and Phasael, who were tetrarchs (41 B.C.). Finally, Herod [the Great] was appointed king of Judea by the Roman senate in 37 B.C. He would stay in power until his death in 4 B.C.

Augustus (Gaius Julius Caesar Octavianus, 63 B.C.–A.D. 14). Under his rule (27 B.C.–A.D. 14) the Roman Empire was firmly established. He was the son of the senator Gaius Octavius, and the great-nephew of Julius Caesar, through his mother Atia. When Caesar was assassinated (44 B.C.) and his will was read, it was discovered that Octavius had inherited his money and his name. Despite the forming of the so-called Second Triumvirate (Octavian, Mark Antony, and Lepidus), civil war erupted for many years to come. Tired of war, the people desired peace, which Augustus was able to bring finally by defeating Antony at the Battle of Actium in 31 B.C. Now secure in power, Augustus was able to initiate many reforms in the Senate and elsewhere. A large part of the army was reduced and the resources saved were given to private investments. Morality was encouraged among the general population by the building of temples to the various gods. To consolidate the empire at large, Augustus decided to take a census of the population in order to tax it more efficiently. Joseph and Mary were among those who were counted (Luke 2). Augustus also fortified the defense of the frontiers of the Roman borders to secure people against hostile forces. In Rome, a police and fire department of civilians was organized to protect the grain supply. Augustus would boast that he had "found Rome brick and left it marble." During his long reign of 41 years, he brought order out of chaos, instilled peace, and presided over a solid administration. In gratitude, in 2 B.C. the Romans gave him the title *Pater Patriae*, Father of his Country. When Augustus (lit. *sacred*) died, the Senate made him a god (*Divus Augustus*).

Tiberius (Julius Caesar Augustus, 42 B.C.–A.D. 37). At the death of Augustus, his adopted son Tiberius, whose mother was Livia, was chosen to reign (A.D. 14–37). At 56 years of age, he was not new to politics. Conservative by nature, he was willing to let previous policies stand when new decisions would have better served the empire. As a result, the armies of Rome suffered defeats in Germany. At home, troubles prevailed because in his personality Tiberius was distant, arrogant, suspicious, and temperamental. Following the untimely death of his heir, Germanicus (A.D. 19), he was more unpopular than ever. People suspected him of murder. In A.D. 26, Tiberius retired to the island of Capri, leaving the government in the hands of the city prefect. His absence gave Aelius Sejanus, the captain of the Praetorian Guard, the incentive needed to initiate a coup. The attempt to take political control of the government was discovered and Sejanus was executed (A.D. 31). A reign of terror followed so that very few people mourned the death of Tiberius in A.D. 37.

Caligula (Gaius Caesar, A.D. 12–41) was chosen by the Senate to rule Rome after the death of Tiberius. He reigned from A.D. 37–41. Having been brought up in an army camp, he was affectionately called "Little Boots" by the army. Caligula was at first very popular as he pardoned political prisoners, reduced taxes, and provided for public entertainment. In time he became lavish, authoritarian, and vicious. He raided the public treasury and then tried to collect more money by confiscating private property, using methods of extortion, and selling political offices. He became mentally unbalanced. The seriousness of his mental condition was manifested by his mandate to be worshipped as a god. When the Jews refused to do this, Caligula ordered that his statue be erected in the Temple at Jerusalem. A general blood bath was averted when the imperial guards assassinated Caligula in AD 41.

Claudius (10 B.C.– A.D. 54) was the grandson of the Empress Livia, brother of Germanicus, and nephew of the Emperor Tiberius. For the early part of his life, Claudius was kept out of sight because of his physical disabilities. An early childhood illness had left him unattractive and with a drooling mouth. Mentally, however, Claudius was very bright. After the death of Caligula, the Praetorian Guard selected Tiberius Claudius Germanicus as the next emperor. He would rule from A.D. 41

to A.D. 54 and prove to be a capable, progressive ruler. As a student of history, he was prepared for the vicious in-fighting of the imperial court. Under Claudius, Rome became a bureaucracy which was governed by committees and secretaries. The borders of Rome were expanded as the army was sent to Britain. Mauretania and Thrace were annexed. In the area of religion, Claudius was determined to restore the ancient Roman gods. This led him to expel from the city of Rome all the Jews because of some riots that had taken place (note Acts 18:2). In A.D. 54 Claudius died. It was widely believed that he was poisoned by his fourth wife, Agrippina the Younger. He left the imperial throne to a monster of a man named Nero.

Nero (Claudius Caesar, A.D. 37–68) was the natural son of Agrippina the Younger (daughter of Germanicus) and the adopted son of Claudius. His original name was Lucius Domitius Ahenobarbus. When Claudius died (A.D. 54), Nero became emperor. The first five years of Nero's reign were peaceful and successful due to the advice of the philosopher Seneca, the Praetorian Prefect, Burrus, and his mother. But suddenly the violence began. Tired of being influenced by his mother, in A.D. 59 Nero had Agrippina murdered in order to take full charge of the government. Without any restraining influence on his life, Nero turned to sex, singing, acting, and the racing of chariots. Losing interest in government, Nero became anxious to perform upon the public stage. Being irresponsible with the public funds, he used violence to re-establish the money supply. The Senate grew to hate Nero as much as the general public. When a great fire broke out in Rome in A.D. 64 and destroyed a large part of the city, Nero, in order to divert blame from himself, accused the Christian community of starting the destruction. Peter and Paul, caught up in the madness of the moment, were put to death. The continuing excesses of Nero led to the Conspiracy of Piso (A.D. 65), which was discovered and put down. Three years later, another major revolt proved successful. Nero fled Rome and was forced to commit suicide.

Galba (Servius Sulpictus Galba, c. 3 B.C.–A.D. 69). The revolt of the legions against Nero manifested the fact that the fate of the empire was in the hands of the army—apart from the will of the Senate. In the army there were many strong-willed and capable men who wanted to be emperor. One such person was Galba. Though enjoying an excellent record as governor in Gaul, Germany, Africa, and Spain during the Julio-Claudian Era, Galba would prove to be a terrible emperor. He was mean and capricious. After only a few months in office, Galba was murdered in a palace coup led by Otho, his former supporter who had persuaded the Praetorian Guard to kill Galba and to make him emperor.

Otho (Marcus Salvius Otho, A.D. 32–69) was the second Roman Emperor in the Year of the Four Emperors (A.D. 69). A former drinking companion of the emperor, Otho governed in Spain until Nero's death (A.D. 68). Initially a supporter of Galba, he organized a coup against him in January of A.D. 69. He became emperor with the backing of the Praetorian Guard, only to find his own power challenged by Vitellius, the governor of Lower Germany. In the civil war that followed, Otho was defeated. He committed suicide in April of A.D. 69.

Vitellius (Aulus Vitellius, A.D. 15–69) was the third of the four emperors who ruled Rome during the Year of the Four Emperors (A.D. 69). Appointed by Galba as Governor of Lower Germany in A.D. 68, he was proclaimed emperor by his troops in January, A.D. 69, but did not actually come to power until April of that year. Once in power, Vitellius was recognized by the Senate, but could not manage his own soldiers nor establish a permanent government. Civil war erupted when the armies of the east intervened in the affairs of state and proclaimed their general, Vespasian, emperor. At the time, Vespasian was engaged in the siege at Jerusalem in an attempt to put down the Jewish revolt that had broken out in the summer of A.D. 66. Willing to leave his son Titus in charge of that situation, Vespasian went to Egypt where he was able to gain control of the country and cut off the food supply of Rome. In the civil conflict that followed, Vespasian's soldiers were able to capture the city of Rome so that Vespasian could be proclaimed ruler.

Vespasian (Titus Flavius Vespasianus, A.D. 9–79). This Roman Emperor (A.D. 69–79) was the founder of the Flavian Dynasty (A.D. 69–96). As a ruler, Vespasian proved to be conservative in his habits and energetic in his administration. He ended the civil wars of Rome by brutally putting down revolts among the Gauls and among the Jews at Jerusalem. He strengthened the frontiers by reducing dependent principalities to the status of provinces, put the empire on a sound financial footing by imposing new taxes, and built the famous Coliseum. Vespasian died in A.D. 79 leaving the throne to his son Titus.

Titus (Flavius Vespasianus, A.D. 39–81) was the elder son and successor of Vespasian. He ruled as emperor of Rome from A.D. 79–81. Though Titus reigned only a short while, he was immensely popular for his generosity, charm, and military victories. Titus sponsored magnificent public entertainment and was generous to the Senate. During his reign, Mount Vesuvius exploded in A.D. 79 which destroyed Pompeii and Herculaneum, villages on the Bay of Naples. Several months later fire broke out in Rome and destroyed the new Capitol, the Pantheon, and Agripp's Baths. Titus responded to these tragic events by building new buildings, including a large amphitheater.

Domitian (Titus Flavius Domitianus, A.D. 51–96) ruled as the Roman Emperor from A.D. 81–96. He was the younger son of Vespasian, and the last of the Flavian emperors. A man with unbridled personal appetites, Domitian tried to promote a higher public ethical level by restraining the corruption of the Roman state and by regulating prostitution. The temples of the old Roman gods were rebuilt. Foreign religions were suppressed, which led to Christian persecution. Becoming increasingly paranoid and growing self-centered, Domitian demanded worship for himself. Ultimately, Domitian made a multitude of enemies including members of his own family. Caught up in a reign of terror in Rome which Domitian unleashed, he was finally assassinated.

Nerva (A.D. 96–98). Nerva was selected by the Senate of Rome to succeed Domitian as emperor. Advanced in years, Nerva had a pleasing disposition and was regarded as harmless. Knowing that his reign would be brief, Nerva arranged for his successor to be the well-respected general Trajan, who was capable of maintaining the loyalty of his troops while administering a fair government with a forceful hand.

Trajan (A.D. 98–117). Nerva died in A.D. 98, and Trajan succeeded him. A Spaniard by birth, a soldier by choice, forceful in temperament and tireless in energy, Trajan ruled well. During his reign, new territory was added to the empire. He died in Cilicia in A.D. 117.

The Consolidation of Control

The ability to maintain an outward expansion and impose Roman authority and government into new territory is found in the provincial system which Rome retained from her Etruscan past. The word *provincia*, from which "province" is derived, is a military word. It was used of the office of carrying on war, or of holding a post or command. The undergirding concept was that military authority was extended to the physical sphere of any territory that a general would subdue. This area became his *provincia*. Each new province which was conquered by the armies of Rome became part of the imperial system regardless of its former size or governmental structure. By using this provincial method, the empire of Rome was able to grow in small and large segments at a time.

Once an area was brought under the sphere of Roman influence, there were two forms of the provincial government. Those provinces or territories that remained peaceful and offered no opposition to Rome were placed under a Roman official called a *proconsul* (Acts 13:7). The proconsuls were held personally accountable to the Roman Senate and were appointed on an annual basis.

The more disorderly provinces were placed directly under the command of the Emperor who ruled by martial law. Armies were located in the areas of occupation. The political administration was conducted by *prefects* (mayors), *procurators* (governors), and *proprietors* (local officials) who held office as long as an emperor was pleased to provide a given post. Under these administrative officials, the inhabitants of the conquered provinces were permitted a certain amount of freedom and local autonomy under the guidance of the *curiates* or city-fathers. They could mint coins and worship as they chose.

The rulers of Rome were inclined to follow the suggestions of the provincial councils on bureaucratic decisions. However, there were checks and balances. Any Roman official who was found guilty of abuse of power was subject to indictment and recall. While this did not eliminate corruption, it did reduce it. Meanwhile common roads were constructed, buildings were erected, and business was developed. In order to guarantee Roman authority in the provinces, small settlements of Romans were started at strategic centers in the provinces. A pattern of uniformity displayed Roman influence.

Each provincial city was laid out according to a common grid-pattern. Each had a forum, temples to the gods, a theater, and baths. In addition, the imperial cult was established whereby people pledged themselves to honor the emperor and even worship him when he desired. Caligula, Nero, Domitian, and Commodus demanded divine honors in their lifetime and received it. Citizens of the empire erected for them statues with the attributes of gods. They offered sacrifices in honor of the emperors and provided them with divine titles.

The Problem of Paganism

Though Rome circled the Mediterranean Sea by military might and diplomatic maneuvering, much of society did not fully enjoy the spoils of victory. A universal military mind-set administered by dictatorial mandates is not conducive to cultivating a philosophy of compassion to helping the poor. Nor does it foster a readiness to return land to its original owners. Greed was considered good in the Roman world. The rich were able to become richer through government control of land; the poor could only get poorer. Despite their wealth, the rich and the rulers of the classical world did not sleep well. Some of the Roman emperors had large mirrors installed at strategic spots in their palaces in order to detect potential assassins. Tiberius may have died from unnatural causes as his four successors certainly did.

The middle class almost disappeared. It could not compete with war, conscription, and cheap labor. In time, the streets of Rome became filled with those who had no job, no home, and little food. There was great social unrest. The *plebian* (poor) people were willing to follow any strong leader who promised to help their plight. Class division was intense. Individuals lived by their wits. Children were encouraged to be wicked and morally corrupt.

In addition to the poor, a large proportion of the population of the Roman Empire consisted of slaves. It has been estimated that less than half of the inhabitants of the Roman Empire were free men, and not all of them were citizens with full legal rights. New military conflicts, personal and national debt, and indiscriminate births enlarged the ranks of the slave population at a rapid rate.

Cultural Achievements

Law and Engineering

In these two practical areas the Romans eventually excelled. Especially in the second and third centuries A.D., the jurisconsults began the accumulation of legal commentary that would serve the European world well in the centuries to come. Taking advantage of the availability of slaves, the Romans were able to combine their technological advances with cheap labor to produce impressive works of hydraulic engineering. They built enduring bridges, aqueducts, theaters, and baths. After inventing concrete and the vaulted dome, the Romans revolutionized the structure and shape of buildings. Volume and lighting suddenly became part of the architectural design and thinking. The Romans learned how to use the principle of the arch to produce a pleasing outcome. Later, the Christian community would find ways to teach spiritual symbolism in the spaces of the great cathedrals they would build.

Literature

Despite the open debauchery that characterized much of Roman life, there were cultural attainments during this period. Under the emperor Augustus, a renaissance in literature was enjoyed, reflected in the poet Vergil. In his work *Aeneid*, Vergil set forth the divine beginning and future of the Roman Empire after presenting an idyllic picture of primitive Rome. Horace and Ovid made their poetical contributions. The Stoic moralist Seneca wrote philosophical essays and tragic drama. A lady of wealth and leisure named Petronius gave the world a novel which is still useful for understanding ordinary life in Roman society. In the latter part of the first century, Pliny the Elder recorded with care his *Natural History*, which is one of the first attempts to objectively observe and categorize life in the natural world. Quintilian studied grammar and rhetoric, while Martial wrote the more sensational news of the day. Suetonius and Tacitus were capable historians. Tacitus wrote his *Annals* and *Histories* and by so doing became an unwitting witness to the fulfillment of the prophetic words of Christ concerning the destruction of Jerusalem. The satirist Juvenal was a severe judge of the manners and morals of the Romans. He knew that most people did not really believe in the pagan gods, like Mars or Venus. "These things," he wrote, "not even boys believe, except such as are not yet old enough to have paid their penny for a bath." In contrast, early Christians appealed to the pagans on the basis of history, not myth. Clement of Rome wrote about Jesus,

> "He that satisfied five thousand men with five loaves and two fishes . . . will raise the dead. For we testify all these things con-

cerning Him. . . . we who have eaten and drunk with Him, and have been spectators of His wonder-filled works and of His life."

Music and Drama

Music and drama were designed to entertain the masses rather than to stimulate any serious creative thinking. The public performances were often found to be obscene, repulsive and crude. Music was "popular."

The Arena

In the great cities of Rome, overshadowing civilization itself in all public places, was the Arena. In the Arena, brutality and butchery mingled with blood and violence against the background of the mighty screams of the masses. Unspeakable personal contests took place between men and beasts or between men and men. These events were allowed, in part, to solidify the people into a Roman culture through cultural urbanization. Another reason was the desire of the rich to display wealth and secure political power. Beginning c. 254 B.C., pretending to be part of something glamorous, prisoners of war, criminals, slaves, and even an emperor engaged in the very popular gladiatorial games despite the gore and shocking savageness of the situation. Spectators showed no mercy to those in the Arena. As the Christian Saturus lay dying from the attack of a leopard, the crowd jeered him with shouts of, "Well washed! Well washed!" referring to the ritual of believer's baptism.

Languages

There were four major languages in the Roman world. There was Latin, the language of the law courts and literature. Latin was spoken in North Africa, Spain, Gaul, Britain and Italy. There was Greek, the common trade language of the people. There was Aramaic, which was the predominate tongue of the Middle East (cp. Acts 22:2; *"abba"* Romans 8:15; *"maranatha"* 1 Corinthians 16:22, and John 19:20). Finally, there was Hebrew, which was really a dead language for practical purposes.

Education

Formal education changed little in practice or content from one century to the next. All educated Romans were bilingual, able to speak Latin and Greek. The training of children in the average Roman household was entrusted to the *paidagogos*, a slave who was responsible for the first lessons (note Gal. 4:1–2). Education took place in the public alcoves, which were halls near the market place and shops of commerce. Rote memorization was emphasized. Lessons were learned through endless repetition. Corporal punishment was frequently administered. The schoolrooms were unimpressive, frigid, and unattractive. The educational curriculum was basic and practical, consisting of reading, writing, arithmetic, Greek and Latin poetry, and oratory.

The Providential Provision of God

As Rome went forth to conquer, the culture of Rome became increasingly influenced by the Hellenistic spirit. This was due in part to the simple fact that the empire had first conquered and then absorbed many Greek colonies which had been established along the seacoasts of Gaul (France) and Spain, on the island of Sicily, and on the mainland of the lower Italian peninsula. With natural pride, the Romans considered themselves the masters, but the Greek "servants" were often the real masters—through the power of education. The Greek slaves became teachers, physicians, accountants, and overseers of farms and businesses. Into the Greek universities of Athens, Rhodes, and Tarsus came young Romans who learned to speak Greek. It has been observed that while the Romans outwardly conquered the bodies of men, the Greeks conquered the minds of all.

The influence of Greek culture was pervasive. It touched all societies including the Jewish community, manifested in the translation of the Hebrew Scriptures into the *Septuagint* during the days of Ptolemy Philadelphus of Egypt (285–246 B.C.). The Roman world also adopted

Greek customs and manners, Greek architecture, and the Greek language (*koine*, common) which became the language of the people. This common 'trade language' enabled clear and rapid communication of the gospel of Christ throughout the civilized world.

In the providence of the Lord, the gospel also would be proclaimed freely in a world which, for the moment, enjoyed the *Pax Romana*—the peace of Rome. Individuals could travel from one end of the Mediterranean world to the other without fear. Even before the advent of Christianity, God had sovereignly used Rome to provide for its spread throughout the world.

2

The Conception of Christianity

A Jewish Culture in a Roman World

The Jewish State

Like many other conquered people, the Jews were ready to endure the Roman enslavement and the cultural influences of the Greeks. Jewish leaders knew that any semblance of a political state existed at the mercy of the Romans. They would do the best they could to survive in three ways.

First, most Jews decided as a people to accept their difficult situation as the will of God. Some, called Zealots, were ready to assassinate any Roman at any given opportunity. But for the most part, the Jews recognized the rule of Rome.

Second, the Jews remembered their rich spiritual and political heritage. The children were taught about the Babylonian Exile, the return to Jerusalem, and the fight for freedom under the Hasmoneans (142–37 B.C.).

Then *third*, the Jews kept their Messianic hopes alive by honoring a religion rooted in the *Torah*, the *Targums*, the *Talmud*. The synagogues were looked after by the Sanhedrin, the ruling body consisting of the scribes, Pharisees, and Sadducees.

The Hebrew word *Torah*, normally translated "law," eventually became a title for the *Pentateuch*, the first five books of the Old Testament. Later, the term was expanded to include all of the Scriptures setting forth the revelation from God. As the Hebrew language gave way to the more prevalent use of Aramaic in Palestine, collections of the Old Testament books were translated from Hebrew into Aramaic, along with various Jewish traditions and oral sayings. These were called *Targums*, and were later amplified by the *Talmud*. The *Talmud* reflects the Hebrew civil and canonical thinking of the rabbis from c. 300 B.C. to A.D. 500. The *Talmud* (lit. *teaching*) consists of the *Mishnah*, or traditional oral law concerning the written Law of Moses itself, and the *Gemara*, a commentary on the legal traditions associated with the Law.

Despite being sent into exile as a result of the Babylonian captivity (586 B.C.), members of the Jewish community committed themselves to keeping their faith by establishing local synagogues in place of the holy Temple in Jerusalem. The synagogue (Gk. *synagogue*, lit. *a gathering* or *assembly*) was first established in the homes of the exiles in Babylon (cf. Ezek. 8:1; 20:1–3). After returning from the Exile, these "house synagogues" developed into formal public assembly places of worship and prayer. When ten or more men were present in an area, a synagogue would be constructed for reverence and instruction in the law and the prophets (cf. Luke 4:16–30) through the study of the *Talmud*. Closely associated with the *Talmud* in the services of the synagogue was the *Midrash*. This body of literature records early synagogue sermons in Hebrew and Aramaic, interpreting the Scriptures of the Old Testament. The *Midrash* was widely used from c. 100 B.C. to A.D. 300.

Pharisees, Sadducees, and Scribes

While the Jews waited for the Messiah, rich and poor lived side by side, as did freeman and slave. Some people were virtuous, and some people were criminals. The majority of the people in Palestine were poor, though in Judaism there was a wealthy aristocracy. The aristocracy consisted mainly of the families of the priesthood and the leading rabbis. Their wealth was derived from the business traffic associated with the Temple, such as the sale of animals for sacrifice and the exchange of money. Despite the class division between the rich and the poor, every Jew could hope to be rich towards God by doing good works. Therefore, obedience to the Law was culturally important.

Pharisees

To inspire people to keep the Law, a religious political party arose named the Pharisees (lit. *to be separate*). The Pharisees first emerged during the Maccabean period in the days of John Hyrcanus (134–104 B.C.). Though they had courageously remained faithful to the Lord during the attacks of Antiochus Epiphanes on Jerusalem in 168 B.C., the Pharisees went on to become rigid legalists who spoke often of prayer, repentance, and giving of alms—sometimes in the wrong way without a whole heart toward God (cp. Matt. 23:1–39).

Sadducees

Opposed to the Pharisees were the Sadducees. Descending from Zadok, who was appointed a priest by Solomon (cp. 1 Kings 2:35), the Zadokites became the liberals of their day. As aristocrats, they were worldly-minded priests who observed the letter of the Law, but denied essential truths such as the resurrection and future retribution. The Sadducees embraced Greek culture. They were willing to sacrifice spiritual principles upon the altar of personal gain, and to do business with any barbarian to enhance their enjoyment of earthly things. The worldly existence of the Sadducees infuriated the Pharisees, which in turn caused the whole Hasmonaean kingdom to be weakened politically—in a world that readily devoured smaller countries.

Scribes

Allied with the Pharisees against the Sadducees were the scribes. The primary job of a scribe was to copy the Holy Scripture. This daily working with the sacred text made the scribes very familiar with the Mosaic Law, and so they were also called "lawyers." They grew influential with the people and became teachers too, knowledgeable sources regarding what the law said. Initially the work of the scribes was very important, for there were few copies of the Word of God—they were all copied by hand in Hebrew.

The Hebrew language used square characters for consonants, which were to be read from right to left, with small dots or signs variously attached for vowels. A good memory was extremely important for the reading of Hebrew, because the vowel system was not introduced until the 6th century A.D. It was easy to produce various readings. Consider the two letters "bd" without a vowel symbol. Should the word be "bed," "bad," "bud," or "bid"? Despite variant readings, God has been faithful to preserve His Word so that the variant readings and marginal notes made by the copyists can be recognized and dealt with. Despite variations in the manuscripts, there is a recognized and reliable Hebrew text, known as the Masoretic Text.

The Rise of Christianity

Into this world of culture and cruelty, wealth and waste, military might and mindless mobs came Christianity. It was the "fullness of time." The prophecies of Daniel (9:24–27) and the promises of God (Gen. 3:15) would be realized. Ordinary men and women would be called upon to do extra-ordinary things on behalf of a Man from Galilee, the God-man, the Lord Jesus Christ. He was born of a virgin (Isa. 7:14) in the reign of Augustus (27 B.C.–A.D. 14), according to Luke 2:1. He was reared in obscurity in order to be dramatically displayed as the true Hope of humanity. He was the Light and Life of lifeless men. He was the only One who could and would take away the sins of the world.

Despite the tumult that surrounded the civil rulers of Rome, Christianity survived to grow from an obscure Jewish sect into a major world religion. How this happened is the wonderful story of God's sovereign grace. Apart from the person of Jesus Christ, it simply would not have happened.

He ministered, died, and rose again from the dead in the reign of Tiberius (A.D. 14–37) as per Luke 3:1. Under the guidance and power of the Holy Spirit, the Church grew during the reigns of Claudius (A.D. 41–54) (Acts 18:2) and Nero (A.D. 54–68). Notwithstanding the cultural challenges and political changes taking place, God advanced the spiritual kingdom that Christ came to establish in the hearts of men. When the rulers of the kingdom of this world (Rome) tried to demolish the Lord's kingdom, they were in turn destroyed (cp. Dan. 9:27).

Formation of the New Testament

While the Old Testament had taken many years to formulate, the New Testament Scriptures were written within one hundred years of each other. However, like the Old Testament canon, it would take time until they could be duly considered by church leaders and guided by the Holy Spirit to formulate a canon.

Because of false teachings springing up, and because the Church was being persecuted for possession of a multitude of various writings (Luke 1:1) from the first century, it was necessary for the Church to consider more closely and formally which books should make up the New Testament, i.e. which books were really the inspired "Word of God," and therefore worth dying for.

Writing in the early part of the fourth century, Eusebius of Caesarea stated that some texts were still being debated. By the middle of the fourth century, the *Codex Vaticanus*, a Greek volume of both Old and New Testaments, listed the complete New Testament as it is known today. And in A.D. 367, Athanasius, Bishop of Alexandria, explained in his annual Easter Festal Letter to all the churches and monasteries within his sphere of authority what the Old Testament and the New Testament canon of Scripture should be. By the first part of the fifth century, the consensus of tradition concerning the canon of Scripture was established and honored. Jerome, in a letter written in 414, accepted the New Testament books listed by Athanasius.

A key in understanding the formation of the New Testament canon is that it was never an arbitrary choice based on the decisions of men. Rather, the canon existed as soon as the Spirit led men to write the words from God. But in order for the church community to recognize that which was God-breathed, four criteria were used powerfully by the Holy Spirit among widely dispersed groups to bring unity in the formation of the canon. Inspired books shared these common attributes:

1. authors were in direct contact with Christ or the Apostles;
2. consistency in doctrine, and evidence of being inspired by the Holy Spirit;
3. wide acceptance and use by churches in all regions, under the guidance of the Spirit;
4. produced dynamic changes in lives, as used by the Spirit.

The New Testament canon uniquely meets these criteria; it truly has been formulated by the hand of God!

Mountain Tops

Although every word of Scripture is inspired of God and useful to us (2 Tim. 3:16), there are nevertheless certain passages in the New Testament which are extremely important and powerful for the edification of the believer. Every chapter of every book has something to say to us, but we find ourselves going back again and again to these passages for encouragement or insight. The list here is by no means complete or conclusive, but it represents a starting point for those who are wanting to get more serious in their understanding of the ways of God:

Mountain Tops of the New Testament

The Sermon on the Mount	Matt. 5–7	*ways in Christ's Kingdom*
Christ Teaches His Own	John 14–17	*intimate relationship*
Man's Ruin and Utter Need	Rom. 1–2	*rejection, rebellion*
God's Gracious Redemption	Rom. 3–5	*justification by faith alone*
Identification with Christ	Rom. 6–8	*victorious Christian life*
Authority	Rom. 13	*rebellion vs. submission*
What Love Is	1 Cor. 13	*the greatest gift*
Christ Lives!	1 Cor. 15	*the resurrection*
The Fruit of the Spirit	Gal. 5	*"love, joy, peace..."*
Heavenly Riches	Eph. 1	*inheritance of the saints*
Spiritual Warfare	Eph. 6	*the believer's armor*
Wonderful Work of Christ	Phil. 2	*Christ's humanity & deity*
Fullness of Deity in Christ	Col. 1	*the supremacy of Christ*
The Great "Hall of Faith"	Heb. 11	*examples for encouragement*
Discipline	Heb. 12	*the role of suffering*
Tests of True Faith	1 John	*faith and works*
Worship	Rev. 4-5	*"God Reigneth."*

Books of the New Testament

	Book	**Chapters**	**Date (A.D.)**
Gospels	Matthew	28	c. 58–68
	Mark	16	c. 65 *(prior to)*
	Luke	24	c. 60
	John	21	c. 80–90
History	Acts	28	63
Epistles	Romans	16	58
	1 Corinthians	16	57
	Book	**Chapters**	**Date (A.D.)**

P	2 Corinthians	13	58
A	Galatians	6	54
U	Ephesians	6	62
L	Philippians	4	62
I	Colossians	4	62
N	1 Thessalonians	5	53
E	2 Thessalonians	3	53
	1 Timothy	6	67
	2 Timothy	4	68
	Titus	3	67
	Philemon	1	61
G	Hebrews	13	58
E	James	5	c. 45–61
N	1 Peter	5	c. 60–67
E	2 Peter	3	c. 60–67
R	1 John	5	c. 60–95
A	2 John	1	c. 60–95
L	3 John	1	c. 60–95
	Jude	1	c. 60–67
Prophecy	Revelation	22	Early date: prior to 70 Late date: c. 90–95

3

Behold the Lamb!
The Synoptic Gospels

Good Tidings

Matthew, Mark, and Luke are called the "Synoptic Gospels" because they review the life of Christ from a common point of view (Gk. *sun*, with; *opsis*, seeing). The word "gospel" comes from an Anglo-Saxon word meaning *god spell*, or *good tidings*. This is a literal translation of the Greek *euaggelion* which referred to bringing good news [*euaggelion* has been transliterated into the English *evangel:* evangelism, evangelical, etc.]. A casual reading of the Gospels reveals that there are both similarities and differences. The challenge facing each student of the Scriptures is to harmonize the separate accounts while understanding how each relates to the others. Such an endeavor is reasonable and exciting, for the discovery will be made of how the Lord has blended the biblical narratives to retell the marvelous story of Divine redemption through the shed blood of Christ at Calvary.

Commonality in the Gospels

Because of the parallelisms found in the Gospel narratives, some believe that these records have been extracted from other sources upon which the authors have relied for information. Of course this need not be the case, because the three gospel writers were each inspired by the same

Holy Spirit. He is the One who could prompt them with the same words to use. But even if there were other common texts which they each referred to, such a situation should produce no surprise, because the use of source material is characteristic of the Jewish teaching culture, as reflected in other portions of the Scriptures.

In the Old Testament, reference is made to various writings that are no longer available (Num. 21:14, Josh. 10:13, 1 Chron. 29:29). And in the New Testament, a similar situation exists: there are references to non-biblical sources.

The Apostle Paul in *Acts* offers a quotation from a pagan poet, Aratus or Cleanthes (Acts 17:28). In 1 Corinthians 15:33, the phrase "evil communication corrupts good manners" is also found in an Attic play and is credited to Menander (322 B.C.).

In several of the Epistles there are verses from a song in the early Church as well as summaries of doctrinal statements that the saints circulated (1 Cor. 11:23–25; Eph. 5:14, 19; Col. 1:13–20; 1 Tim. 3:16, 6:15–16).

Titus 1:12 declares that, "the Cretans are always liars, evil beasts, slow bellies." This description also occurs in a hymn to Zeus by Callimachus in Hesiod, and in a writing of Epimenides.

Several suggestions have been offered to explain the many phrases which the Gospels have in common [note: abstracted from William Graham Scroggie's work: *A Guide to the Gospels.*]

The Oral Tradition Hypothesis

It has been argued that each of the Evangelists wrote independently of the others, relying solely upon what they remembered about the words and works of Christ. Because they were with Him for so long and often repeated what was done, the stories about Jesus are fixed and reliable. It would not be illogical to believe that the oral traditions would have arisen in Jerusalem (cp. Luke 1:4 RV) and been preserved until the events could be written (Luke 1:1). According to Divine design, the truth of the Gospel was entrusted to the care of faithful Christian converts with good memories aided by the Holy Spirit (John 14:26). This view cannot be easily dismissed, for the life of Christ would make a deep impression upon anyone. The Jews were very familiar with catechetical schools which trained the memory and preserved oral traditions.

The Mutual-Use Hypothesis

Another view is that the similarities of the gospels can be attributed to the fact that the writers of the Gospels simply used each other's writings. However, it is not certain who might have borrowed from whom.

The Documents Hypothesis

Some Bible scholars believe that there are at least two documents that were used in the writing of the synoptic gospels. The first source is the *Gospel of Mark*. The argument states that Mark wrote his gospel first and that Matthew and Luke borrowed extensively from it. Of the 1,068 verses (RV) found in *Matthew*, about 500 are from *Mark's* 661 verses; and of *Luke's* 1,149 verses (RV), about 320 are from *Mark*. In summary, there are only about 55 verses of *Mark* not to be found in *Matthew* or *Luke*.

While some scholars believe that Matthew and Luke borrowed from Mark, others believe that the apostles either consulted or borrowed from a now non-existent document which is called "Q," so designated from the German *quelle*, which means "source." The main problem is that the biblical critics are not in agreement upon the contents of Q. Nor is there any common consent as to how much of this hypothetical document each of the Evangelists might have used. One main reason why a Q document is even considered is because Papias, Bishop of Hierapolis (A.D. 130), made an obscure statement that, "Matthew composed [i.e., put together in writing] the Oracles [of Jesus] in the Hebrew [Aramaic?] and each one interpreted them as he was able" (Eusebius, *Historia Ecclesiae*, III. 39).

The idea that there might have been a common collection of the sayings of Christ, called the *Oracles* or *Logia,* finds support from Irenaeus in the second century, by Origen in the third, and by Eusebius in the fourth (*Church Fathers*, p. 39). In the end, it should be noted that the Documents Hypothesis based upon parallel passages is only a theory and is not a certainty. Therefore, it should be considered with reservation.

While it is not necessary, or even desirable, for the average student of the Bible to go into all the complexities of textual criticism, a Christian should not be ignorant of the fact that legitimate concerns about biblical documents do exist. There is merit in the technical examinations of the data behind the Gospels provided by Source-Criticism and Form-Criticism. For this study, it is enough to remember that, "The evangelist was not the compiler of a history, but the missionary who carried the good tidings to fresh countries; the bearer, and not the author of the message" (Bishop Westcott). Also, it should not be forgotten that all three Gospels revolve around the Person and work of the Lord Jesus Christ, whose ministry would not soon be forgotten by those who were intimately associated with Him. It might be more surprising if the Gospels were not so close in harmony.

The Gift of the Gospels

By acknowledging the possibility of source documents, nothing is taken away from the doctrine of divine inspiration, nor from the truth that the Gospels were produced independently, at different times, in different places, and for different purposes. Each Gospel has its own characteristics, emphasis, and personal expression as Jesus Christ is presented in all of His splendor and glory.

Matthew	Mark	Luke	John
Messiah	Servant	Perfect Man	Son of God
Jewish world	Roman world	Greek world	All the world
authority	ministry	integrity	Deity
what Jesus *said*	what Jesus *did*	what Jesus *thought*	what Jesus *was*
sermons	miracles	parables	personal interviews

It is not known for certain where or when the Gospels were first made available to the general public. The letters of Ignatius (A.D. 70–115, bishop of Antioch) provide the earliest quotations in the *Epistle of Barnabas*, the *Teachings of the Twelve Apostles*, and the *Epistle of Polycarp*. These documents all relate to the church at Antioch of Syria. If, as Papias believed, *Matthew* was first written for the Hebrew [Aramaic] church in Jerusalem, then this Gospel would have been read soon after A.D. 50 and prior to the fall of Jerusalem in A.D. 70.

According to Clement of Alexandria (A.D. 200) and Irenaeus (c. A.D. 100), Mark wrote his gospel after the death of Peter. If the second gospel records the memories of Peter, then it was probably put in circulation c. A.D. 65.

The *Gospel of Luke* may have originally been intended to be a private document to the friends of Luke such as Theophilus (Luke 1:3). It may have been prior to A.D. 62 in light of *Acts*, which was written near the end of the first imprisonment of Paul. It is possible that *John* was written prior to A.D. 50, though a later date (c. A.D. 85) is often given.

A Concise Summary of the Life of the Lord Jesus Christ

5 B.C.	Angelic appearance to Zacharias
6 months later	Angelic appearance to Mary
	Mary visits Elizabeth
3 months later	Mary returns to Nazareth
	Angelic appearance to Joseph
	Birth of John the Baptist
4 B.C.	Birth of Jesus Christ
	Angelic appearance to the shepherds
8 days later	Jesus is circumcised
32 days later	Jesus is presented in the Temple
3 B.C.	The visit of the Wise Men
	The flight into Egypt
	The slaughter of the Innocents
2 B.C.	The return to Nazareth
A.D. 26 Fall	Baptism in the Jordan River
	Wilderness temptation
	The calling of the first of the disciples
A.D. 27	Jesus cleanses the Temple in Jerusalem
1st Passover	Ministers for eight months in Judea (cp. John 3:22–36)
December	Travels through Samaria to begin the Great Galilean Ministry, lasts for two years
	Performs His first miracle at Cana
	Heals the son of a nobleman at Capernaum
	Returns to Nazareth only to be rejected
	Moves to Capernaum where he calls Peter and Andrew, James and John
	Heals a demoniac and many others

	Matthew is called to follow Christ
	Questions are answered about fasting and the Sabbath
A.D. 28	Jerusalem is visited (John 5:1)
2nd Passover	Jesus heals on the Sabbath despite opposition
	Asserts He is 'very God' and returns to Galilee
Summer	All of the Twelve are finally chosen
	The Sermon on the Mount is preached
	Many parables and miracles, including the raising of Jairus' daughter from the dead.
	Accused of being in harmony with Beelzebub
	Resurrects the widow of Nain's son
	Receives a question from John the Baptist
	Visits Nazareth once more
	Heals the servant of a centurion
	Forgives a woman of her sin
A.D. 29	The Twelve Apostles are sent to preach
February	John the Baptist is murdered
	The Twelve Apostles return
3rd Passover	The 5,000 are fed
	Discourses on the Bread of Life
	Performs many miracles
	Discourses on defilement
	Cities are condemned
	Retires to the north
	Heals a Syro-Phoenician woman
	Returns to Galilee
	Feeding of the 4,000
	Gives the sign of Jonah as His resurrection
	Heals a blind man
October	Jerusalem is visited (John 7:2, 10)

	Forgives woman taken in adultery
	Blind man healed
	Condemns the religious rulers
November	Returns to Galilee
	Peter makes his great confession
	The Transfiguration takes place
	Heals a boy with epilepsy
December	The Galilean Ministry is concluded (Luke 9:51)
	The journey to Jerusalem (John 10:22)
	The Judean and Perean Ministries take place, lasting 4 to 6 months
	The Lord foretells His death three times
	The Lord answers the question of greatness
A.D. 30	Leaves Galilee for Jerusalem
	Lazarus is raised from the dead
4th Passover	The Triumphal Entry into Jerusalem
Last week	Cleansing the Temple
	Teaching in the Temple
	Arrest and Trials
	The Lord is crucified and buried
	On the third day, He rose again!

4

The King and His Kingdom

THE GOSPEL ACCORDING TO MATTHEW

Written c. 58–68
Key word: "King"

"Tell ye the daughter of Sion, 'Behold, thy King cometh unto thee, meek...'"
—Matthew 21:5

Why Written: Presenting Christ as the King of the Jews

It was Matthew's desire to use the knowledge he had of the history and honored tradition of his people. He wanted to help the Jews see that Christ was the fulfillment of all the Old Testament prophecies. At least 60 times Matthew will appeal to the Old Testament Scriptures as being confirmation of the validity of the Person and work of Jesus Christ, including born of a virgin in Bethlehem, His suffering, "hung on a tree," and the Triumphal Entry into Jerusalem. Matthew proclaims to the Jewish nation that Jesus is their long-awaited Messiah, their King. In so doing, he lays a solid historical foundation for all believers today.

Without using the term per se, Matthew describes the Lord much as "the Lion of the tribe of Judah" (Rev. 5:5). The lion represents royalty, majesty, strength, and authority; indeed, Christ is the King of the Jews.

Matthew traces the Lord's genealogy to show Him as rightful heir to the throne of David. In the five discourses, the new covenant of our Lord's kingdom is set forth.

Leaving All to Follow the Lord

Though he was ordained by God to eternal life, converted by the Holy Spirit, and called by Christ to Christian service (Rom. 8:29–30), little is known of the man named Matthew (lit. "gift of God") from his own gospel. That is not bad, for it is one of the measures of a virtuous man that he does not speak of himself but of his Lord and Savior (cp. John 3:30). We do know that Matthew was probably a Galilean and born at or near Capernaum. He was the son of Alphaeus and Mary, who may have been a relative of Mary, the mother of Christ. But best of all, we know that Matthew met the Master.

The power of the pen would serve Matthew well as an author, for as a person he was not well received in religious society. Matthew had disgraced himself. By becoming a tax collector, he had dishonored the ancient beliefs and behavior that for centuries had helped the Jewish nation survive foreign domination. He became a man whom other men despised, for he conspired with the enemy. Matthew had become a collector of Roman revenue.

The Roman officials who were directly responsible to extract money from the people were called "publicans" (from the Latin *publicanus*) because of their close proximity to the purses of the public. The Jews deeply resented any one of their own nation who accepted the office of publican, for such a person was a traitor with God and man. Though a publican might become wealthy, he was cast outside the boundaries of decent society, and was relegated by the righteous to be among the "sinners."

In the territory under the jurisdiction of Herod Antipas, Matthew became a custom's official. He sat at a specific location in Capernaum on the Sea of Galilee and made money simply by extracting excessive taxes from his own countrymen who passed by. There was much money to be made, for Capernaum was along the important caravan route that came from Egypt and led all the way to Damascus and the Mesopotamia Valley in the north.

Why did Matthew do such a thing? He did not have to work for Rome. He did not have to be a social outcast. According to Mark and Luke his name was Levi (lit. "joined"; cp. Mark 2:14; Luke 5:27) which indicates that he was of a priestly line. Matthew should have been set apart for the work and service of God (Num. 3:6; Deut. 10:8). Instead, he chose to serve man and mammon.

John the Baptist had warned against this. When some publicans came to ask him the way into the kingdom of heaven, John had instructed them to repent of their sins and to, "Exact no more than that which is appointed you" (Luke 3:12,13).

One day, while sitting at the receipt of custom, a shadow fell across Matthew's path. He looked up to see who stood in his way. That upward look changed Matthew forever, for he gazed into the face of the Son of the Living God. Jesus said simply enough, "Follow Me" (Matt. 9:9). Matthew got up and he followed Christ all the way to Calvary, and beyond that, into immortality.

Because Matthew committed himself fully to the Lord, he gave his life to bring others to faith. This is reflected in the fact that soon after conversion, Matthew held a great dinner party where he introduced others to the Lord (9:10, cp. Luke 5:29). Then for over three years Matthew listened as Jesus expounded the Scriptures. He watched the miracles of the Master, and what he witnessed Matthew never forgot.

The Message, not the Man

His memory served him well, for the time came when he picked up a pen and began to write the life of Christ under the influence of the Holy Spirit (2 Tim. 3:16). There is a strong early tradition that Matthew initially wrote his gospel in Hebrew for the nation of Israel, which means that he probably wrote in Aramaic, the spoken language of his day (*Historia Ecclesiastica*, Eusebius, A.D. 264–340). Unfortunately, no trace of this first edition of Matthew's gospel has survived. What has survived is the gospel in Greek dating back to the second half of the first century.

Little is known of the life of Matthew following the end of the earthly ministry of Christ. It is possible that he preached in Palestine and then traveled to Persia, Media, and Parthia before becoming a martyr for Christ in Ethiopia. According to *Foxe's Book of Martyrs*, Matthew was killed with a battle ax in the city of Nadabah, A.D. 60.

Overview of Matthew

With the enabling of the Holy Spirit to recall the specific words of Christ, Matthew presents in a very logical way the great themes associated with the ministry of the Lord. He collects many of the most notable parables of the Savior. Matthew also is careful to set forth five selected sermons, or discourses, as a main emphasis of his Gospel, using these as the framework for presenting the teachings of Christ. Surrounding these great sermons are other important details of the life of Christ.

Sermon	**Chapters**
The Sermon on the Mount	5—7, *Character of the Kingdom*
Instruction to the Twelve	10, *Proclaiming the Kingdom*
Mysteries of the Kingdom	13, *Parables on the Kingdom*
Significance of Humble Service	18, *Fellowship in the Kingdom*
Woes and the Olivet Discourse	23—25, *The end of the Kingdom*

Particular attention should be given to Christ as *King* in Matthew's gospel, for this gospel is designed to present Christ to the Jew—first as King, and then as the Savior (cf. John 1:11–12). The late Bible teacher J. Vernon McGee has a helpful outline:

Section	Chapters
Person of the King	1—2, *Birth*
Preparation of the King	3—4:16, *John the Baptist*
Proclamation of the King	4:17—9, *Sermon on the Mount*
Program of the King	10—20, *Teachings, Miracles*
Passion of the King	21—28, *The last week*

Person of the King (1—2)

The narrative begins with the genealogy of the Messiah, "the son of David." It is divided into three equal sections of fourteen generations each (1:17). The threefold division harmonizes with the periods before, during, and after the occupation of the throne by the lineage of David. It is important to note that while Matthew traces the genealogy of Christ from Abraham to Joseph, emphasis is made on the royal descent from David through Solomon. In Luke's genealogy, the ancestry of Jesus is traced back to David through the house of Nathan (Luke 3:23-38).

The purpose of this twofold lineage is to demonstrate that Christ has a legal right to the throne of Israel. In all the charges brought against the Lord during His ministry, no one ever accused Him of not being of the royal line of David. The genealogy proves that Jesus was born the legal King of the Jews, a true "son of David," and thus a son of Abraham. He was conceived by the Holy Spirit (1:18-25), demonstrating that He was the Son of God, and very God of very God (cp. John 1:1-2)—while still a man (cp. Luke 1:26-35; 2:1-7; John 1:14) in fulfillment of the prophecy of Isaiah (7:14, cf. Matt. 1:22-23).

The genealogy of Christ is followed by the story of His birth, the worship of the Wise Men, the murderous intent of Herod the Great, the flight into Egypt, and the return to Nazareth. The "Wise Men" refer to the Magi, a group of scholarly men of Persia. Following a supernatural astronomical phenomenon, they were brought to worship the King of kings and Lord of lords, not on the night of His birth, but when He was a young child (cp. Matt. 2:11).

Warned of God not to report back to the cruel Idumaean named Herod, who ruled Judea as king by the authority of the Roman senate (from 37 B.C. to 4 B.C.), the Wise Men departed into their own country another way (Matt. 2:12). Their gifts of gold (reflecting deity), frankincense (reminding one of prayer), and myrrh (used in embalming the dead) would serve to remind the Savior's parents of their Son's coming hour of sacrifice (note Luke 2:19).

Preparation of the King (3—4:16)

Passing over the youthful years of the Lord, Jesus is suddenly presented for public ministry against the background of the preaching of John the Baptist, His own baptism, and His temptation by Satan. During the following two years (of the Galilean ministry), Capernaum on the Sea of Galilee will serve as point of return and departure in fulfillment of the prophecy of Isaiah 9:1.

The preaching of John, which had been predicted in the Old Testament (cf. Isa. 40:3–5; Mal. 3:1), is described by Luke (1:5–80) as preparatory work for the Messiah. What a privilege it was for John to baptize the Lord in order for Him "to fulfill all righteousness" (Matt. 3:15), the righteousness of the Mosaic Law. The Levitical law required that all priests be consecrated by ritual purification (Ex. 29:4–7; Lev. 8:6–36) when they "began to be about thirty years of age" (Luke 3:23; cf. Num. 4:3). Though Jesus was without sin, He was the fulfillment of all the types and shadows which spoke of Him, and so He graciously identified Himself with sinners.

Following His baptism, Jesus was tested of the devil. His total reliance upon the Father and the Word of Truth (cf. Deut. 8:3; 6:16; 10:20) made Him worthy as the Sinless One to bear the sins of the unrighteous in His own body.

Proclamation of the King (4:17—9)

During the Galilean ministry, Jesus will call His twelve Apostles, preach the Sermon on the Mount, and perform great miracles—He is proclaiming His kingdom to the Jews. The King of the kingdom will not only speak, but He will demonstrate His great authority over all manner of demons and diseases. Even the winds and the sea will obey Him! Best of all, the King has the authority to forgive sin.

In the *Sermon on the Mount*, the greatest sermon ever spoken, the Lord sets forth His ethical teachings, which are binding on all believers in all ages without exception. Jesus made it clear that the externals of the Mosaic Law were to be applied to the heart—a much stronger requirement (able to be met only through Christ). Those who are true citizens of the kingdom of heaven will learn the way to spiritual blessings, out of a motive of love—not in order to earn salvation. The heirs of the kingdom will learn how to pray, and how to live out the normal Christian life in a way that is pleasing to the Lord. And here we have our first introduction to the Lord's marvelous use of word pictures from everyday life in order to make striking and penetrating spiritual applications. Sometimes they were simple metaphors, sometimes they were simply object lessons, and sometimes they were put into stories called *parables*.

Program of the King (10—20)

Chapters 10—16:20

Once the Twelve disciples have been prepared for ministry, the Lord will send them on a mission with instruction on how to preach. The need for more laborers will be stressed. During their missionary journey, the disciples were to go only to the lost sheep of the house of Israel. They were not to go among the Gentiles nor to enter into the towns of the Samaritans—the gospel would first be offered to Israel. The disciples were given power to perform miracles in order to confirm that they were true Ambassadors of Christ.

Despite the preaching of the gospel and the performing of great miracles, most of the people did not come to faith in Christ. A judicial judgment was passed upon some towns such as Chorazin, located 2 miles north of Capernaum, and Bethsaida (lit. "houses," i.e., places of catching fish).

Later, the scribes and the Pharisees, who had been hostile to the Lord from the first, began to discuss openly how they could destroy Him. When companies of scribes and Pharisees from Jerusalem came down to Galilee to unite with His enemies there, Jesus rebuked all of them, declaring them to be blind leaders and hypocrites!

While He ministered on the shores of the Sea of Galilee, the Lord's mother and brothers and sisters went to see Him. But they did not understand His ministry and left (12:46–50). Later, while visiting His home town of Nazareth for a second time, Jesus was again misunderstood, and was rejected by the rulers of the synagogue (13:53–58).

Even John the Baptist had become concerned. He must have thought that perhaps he, too, had misunderstood the things concerning the Messiah after all. But no, John had not misunderstood. He had met the Master and loved Him. John will die the death of the righteous by the wicked hand of Herod Antipas, a son of Herod the Great. John will be received into heaven as the greatest among men.

Despite all of the doubt and opposition which He encountered, even from family and friends, the Lord continued to perform miracles, such as calming the raging sea. Jesus will continue to teach in parables, feed the hungry (5,000 and then 4,000), show love for the multitudes and prepare for the day of His sacrificial death. The Lord spoke often of His death, while assuring Peter and others that ultimate victory would be found in His resurrection. He told Peter (*petros*, a stone) that the Church will be built upon a rock (*petra*, a great ledge of rock), even Christ (cf. 1 Pet. 2:4–6 with 1 Cor. 3:11).

The parables on the kingdom (chapter 13) and the sermon on humility (chapter 18) bring the Galilean Ministry to a close. Following the

Transfiguration (ch. 17), which took place on Mount Hermon during a visit to Caesarea Philippi, Jesus departed from Galilee. The people left behind had many precious memories. They could consider all that they had seen and heard. They would discuss in detail the meaning of the seven parables (or mysteries) of the kingdom of heaven presented by the Great Teacher (ch. 13).

Chapters 16:21—20

Peter, James, and John left Galilee with the memory of the majesty of Christ being revealed in glory in the Transfiguration (2 Pet. 1:16–21). Such glory will make it easier for those in the kingdom to be characterized by humility (18:1–14), prayer (18:15–20), and the ability to forgive others (18:21–35).

Leaving Capernaum and Galilee, Jesus began the Perean ministry. The time may have been in the summer or early autumn of A.D. 29, six months before the trial and Crucifixion. This particular phase of the ministry took place in the territory of Perea—"beyond" or east of the Jordan. This area extended from the Sea of Galilee on the north to the Dead Sea on the south. Several trips were made by the Lord and the disciples to Jerusalem, including a visit for the celebration of the Feast of the Tabernacles in September, and the Feast of Dedication in December.

During this period, Jesus spoke on the sanctity of marriage (19:1–15). He re-established the high standard against divorce. Even when His disciples were amazed, the Lord did not alter His position. The ethics of the Kingdom are not wanted by all. One rich young man (19:16–26) thought the Lord was asking too much. But there are rewards in regeneration when Jesus rules and reigns for those who follow Him (Matt. 19:27–30).

It was also during this time period that Jesus sent forth the seventy disciples into Judea, who returned with exciting reports of great spiritual results (cp. Luke 10:1–17). While not all disciples will meet with as great results as the seventy sent forth, all will be treated fairly by the Master at the end of the day (Matt. 20:1–16).

The events of this period are treated briefly by Matthew and Mark, with more detail by John, but at great length by Luke (cp. Luke 9:51–19:28). For the fourth time, Jesus predicts His death and resurrection (cf. Matt. 12:38–42; 16:21–28; 17:22–23; 20:17–28).

Passion of the King (21—28)

The last week of the Lord's ministry occupies a great portion of all the gospel narratives. The main episodes of the Last Week include the Triumphal Entry into Jerusalem; the driving of the traders out of the Temple, the story of the widow's mite, the parables of talents and of foolish virgins, the Last Supper, the washing of the feet of the disciples, the various trials, the Crucifixion, the burial, and the glorious Resurrection.

Since so much attention surrounds the death of Christ, careful consideration should be given to the seven trials of the Savior as recorded in the following passages: Matthew 26:57–68; Mark 14:53–65; Luke 22:54, 55, 63–65, 67–71; John 18:24; Matt. 27:1–2; 27:11–26. These trials may be divided between the Ecclesiastical courts and the Civil courts.

The Ecclesiastical trials are three in number: the preliminary hearing before Annas (John 18:12–14, 19–23); the trial before Caiaphas and select members of the Sanhedrin (Matt. 26:57); and the trial before the whole assembled body of the Sanhedrin after daybreak (Matt. 27:1–2) where Jesus is charged with blasphemy (Matt. 26:65).

The Civil trials are three in number: the trial before Pilate (Matt. 27:11–26) whereby Jesus is charged with being a revolutionist, inciting the people not to pay their taxes, and claiming to be a king (Luke 23:2); the trial before Herod Antipas (Luke 23:6–12); and, finally, the return to Pilate for a second trial (Luke 23:11–25).

The seventh trial for the Savior was a Theocratic trial which took place at Calvary, whereby God the Father judged the sins of the world in the Person of His only begotten Son.

The gospel narrative ends with the glorious Resurrection of Christ—*who is alive forevermore!*

5

The Servant of All

THE GOSPEL ACCORDING TO MARK

Written in Rome prior to A.D. 65
Key word: "servant"

"For even the Son of man came not to be ministered unto [served], but to minister [serve], and to give his life a ransom for many."

—Mark 10:45

Why Written: Presenting Christ as Servant of All

While the *Gospel of Mark* is second in the order of the books of the New Testament, it is probable that this work was the first to be written (c. A.D. 56–65). The purpose of the writing was to reach the Roman world with the good news of redemption. To do this, Mark presents Christ as "servant of all" (Mark 10:44). He is "meek and lowly," and "came not to be served, but to serve." The phrase "Son of man" positions Him as a servant. By using a short, jumpy writing style, Mark highlights the often busy schedule of Jesus, moving from one scene to the next with intense activity. A servant is not known by what he says, but by what he does.

Jesus continually gave Himself to the needs of the people—in teaching, healing, and performing miracles. In the entire record, there is not one sentence of His seeking to be served, or even serving Himself. It is all a continuous serving of others, right through the washing of the disciples' feet in the Upper Room. Yet He is always in perfect serenity and control—never frustrated, angry, or reacting in a self-centered way.

The *Gospel of Mark* begins with a fast pace in the baptism of Jesus by John the Baptist. The Lord is about 30 years old. His initial ministry will be concentrated in Galilee and Capernaum where Peter lived. Nothing is said of the Lord's birth, infancy, or childhood, nor of those associated with Him during these early years. While these things are very important, Mark wants to emphasize the service of Jesus and His miracles.

Mark's focus is primarily toward the Roman world. Mark wants to prove that Jesus is the Christ, the Son of God, with power manifested in the mighty miracles He performed. The Romans respected power. They would be impressed with divine authority that could subdue the elements, cause the blind to see, the lame to walk, the deaf to hear, and the dead to live. Mark was anxious to tell the world of Rome about the miracles of the Messiah.

A Young Man of Privilege and Destiny

Mark was uniquely gifted to present Christ to the Roman world, as his life's story reveals. Mark was the son of Mary, known as "Mary of Jerusalem" (Acts 12:12), to distinguish her from four others with the same name. According to Luke, his full name was John Mark (Acts 15:27). Paul and Peter referred to him by his Latin (or Roman) name of Marcus (Col. 4:10; Phil. 1:24; 1 Pet. 5:13).

John Mark came from a wealthy family which enjoyed having its own house and employed servants. But the gifts of God's grace were not used for selfish things. As a follower of the Lord, Mary opened her home to the Christians in Jerusalem (Acts 12:12–17). Some have suggested that the Last Supper was held in the Upper Room of her home.

If the "young man" referred to in this gospel (14:51) is Mark himself, then there was one dreadful night that he never forgot. It was the night Jesus was arrested. As the tragic event began to unfold, there was a great noise in the streets of Jerusalem. John Mark would have been awakened at midnight by the commotion in the courtyards. Draping a linen cloth about his body, he hastily ran outside to discover the terrible situation of the One he knew so well, Jesus. The situation proved overwhelming and terrifying; John Mark fled in fear into the night, along the side of more mature men (14:50).

Despite that tragic moment, John Mark went on to become a disciple of Jesus Christ and himself a supportive "servant" of Peter, Paul, and Barnabas. Perhaps Peter led John Mark to the Lord (cp. 1 Pet. 5:13). As time went on and the gospel began to be taken to other parts of the Roman world, John Mark was honored to join the group of apostles and evangelists who were sent out by the church in Jerusalem to the churches in Judea and Samaria, then to Antioch in Syria, then onward to Ephesus in the West in Asia Minor, and finally to Rome.

Unity, Division, and Reconciliation

The year is A.D. 44. John Mark is found to be a traveling companion of Barnabas and Paul, who have been sent by the church at Antioch with contributions for the suffering saints of Jerusalem following a famine there. Barnabas and Paul arrived safely, delivered the money, and were ready to go back to Antioch when a question arose. Could John Mark travel with them? Of course! And so it was that Barnabas and Paul and John Mark returned to Antioch to preach the gospel with great power and results. Then the Holy Spirit prompted Barnabas and Paul to embark on their First Missionary Journey. In A.D. 45 the adventure began. Could John Mark come with them? Of course!

The missionaries got on board a boat whose sails were set for the islands of Cyprus. From there, the journey would be made to the mainland of Asia Minor in the districts of Pamphylia and Galatia. But then something happened. At the town of Perga, John Mark made a decision to go no further. We know nothing more of his motive, but John Mark withdrew from the pilgrimage and returned to Jerusalem.

A few years later, in A.D. 50, a Second Missionary Journey was proposed. Once more it was suggested that John Mark go along. However, unlike the first time, Paul would not agree. John Mark had deserted them. John Mark had proven unfaithful. John Mark was not to be trusted. Heated words were exchanged between Barnabas and Paul. Passion heated up. Finally, a decision was made. Paul would leave the area with Silas. Barnabas could travel with John Mark to Cyprus.

Twelve years later the story resumes. Nothing has been heard of John Mark during the interval. Suddenly, he appears in two Pauline letters. Whatever differences of opinion there had been, it is obvious that they have been forgiven and forgotten (cp. Col. 4:10 with Philemon 1:24). Writing from a prison cell in Rome c. A.D. 61, Paul refers to John Mark as his companion and fellow-laborer.

The remaining life of John Mark is shrouded with mystery. It is believed that he worked closely with Peter until the apostle met death in A.D. 67. Following the martyrdom of Peter, John Mark, according to legend, became the founder and first bishop of the church in Alexandria, Egypt, the second largest city of the Roman Empire at the time. Whatever his ultimate destiny may have been, it is certain that John Mark has given to the world an authentic gospel of our great God and Savior, Jesus Christ.

The Authenticity of Authorship

The authorship of Mark is attributed to him by Papias, bishop of Hierapolis and a disciple of the Apostle John. Writing c. A.D. 135, Papias quotes an earlier presbyter who stated that Mark was Peter's interpreter.

> Mark, having become the interpreter of Peter, wrote down accurately, though not in order, as many as he remembered of the things said or done by the Lord. For he neither had heard the Lord nor followed Him, but at a later time, as I said, he attached himself to Peter, who delivered his instructions according to the

needs of the occasion, but not with a view to giving a systematic account of the Lord's sayings.[1]

Justin Martyr (early Christian writer and martyr, c. 100–165), Clement of Alexandria (c. 155–220), and Irenaeus (bishop of Lyons in southern France, c. 175–195) also support the position that Mark wrote on Peter's behalf, thereby giving to the world a dramatic narrative of the apostle's early days with Christ.

In addition to the external evidence for Mark writing on behalf of Peter, there is internal evidence (within the book itself). The influence of Peter is pervasive. Three important events illustrate this: the raising of the daughter of Jarius, the Transfiguration, and the prayer of Jesus in Gethsemane. Only James, John, and Peter were present when these events took place. James was soon killed by Herod (Acts 12:2). John wrote an independent gospel. That left only Peter as a reliable source to relate these events, which he did, to John Mark.

Another evidence for Peter's influence upon Mark's gospel is revealed in the fact that the small details recorded by others which made Peter look good are omitted (cp. Mark 8:29 with Matt. 16:17–19), while those moments of the apostle's personal failures are included (note Mark 8:33 and 14:67–72). There are few people who would record for posterity the truth about their moral and spiritual deficiencies.

The greatness of redeeming grace is revealed in the position of humility that Peter takes. One distinguishing characteristic of Mark's gospel is the use of the terms "straightway" and "immediately." These words are used more than 40 times to present a connected narrative of the ministry of Jesus. There is much more chronology in Mark's Gospel than in the Gospels of Matthew and Luke.

---

[1] Eusebius, *Historia Ecclesiae*, III. 39.

Overview of Mark

Following the pattern of all four Gospels, Mark may be grouped into three broad sections: (1) the period before Jesus' public ministry; (2) the three years of public ministry; and, (3) the last week of His physical life on earth. It divides as follows:

Section	Chapters
Sanctification	1:1—1:13, *John the Baptist, Temptation*
Service	1:14—10, *Preaching, Teaching, Miracles*
Sacrifice	11—16, *The last week*

Sanctification (1:1–1:13)

The beginning of the Lord's public ministry is the starting point for Mark's narrative. Jesus is immediately set forth as "the Christ" [Greek: *the Anointed One*, i.e. the Messiah], the Son of God—and thus the incarnate Deity. John the Baptist is declared to be the forerunner of the Messiah according to prophecy (Mal. 3:1, cp. Isa. 40:3). Though the mighty Son of God, the Messiah has come as the Servant of the Sovereign. As the obedient Servant, through the cleansing ritual of baptism, He shall identify Himself with those He has come to seek and to save (cp. Matt. 3:13–17; Luke 3:21–22). The Messiah will be baptized and He will also be tempted by the devil to test His true humanity (cf. Matt. 4:1-11; Luke 4:1-13). He will emerge victorious over Satan (Heb. *Adversary*).

Service (1:14—10)

Chapters 1:14–4:34

Jesus began His Galilean ministry. His main place of residency was in Capernaum on the Sea of Galilee. Twelve apostles were called to be with Him. Many miracles took place in the vicinity of Capernaum amidst rising opposition. The unpardonable sin is discussed (3:20–30). This sin refers to ascribing to Satan the works of God (note Matt. 12:24–37).

Chapters 4:35—9

The Lord expands His Galilean ministry. During a two year period, evangelistic work will be conducted all around the Sea of Galilee. The Lord will preach in Tyre and Sidon. He will move on to the east side of Galilee, and go north to minister to Bethsaida and Caesarea Philippi. His glory will be manifested in the Transfiguration despite growing opposition from the Pharisees. When they challenged Christ by asking for a sign, the Lord spoke harsh words of judgment against them (8:10–21). Finally, the time came when the Lord departed from Galilee. The sovereignty of the Servant over Satan and his spirits was clearly demonstrated.

Demons are fallen angels who have become evil or unclean spirits by rebelling against God's rule and reign (Mk. 1:23 with Mk. 1:32–34; Rev. 16:13–16; Matt. 12:26–27; 25:41). While limited in power, demons can do much damage by inflicting men with diseases. Some angels have been incarcerated until the day of judgment (Jude 6; 2 Pet. 2:4). Many are free to roam the universe for a limited time.

Chapter 10

The Lord spent six months in Perea and Judea. Mark mentions this period only briefly. Perea refers to the area across Jordan from Samaria, extending from the Decapolis east of the Sea of Galilee, and south to the Dead Sea. Herod Antipas ruled this region. Jesus taught on divorce declaring that God designed marriage to be permanent.

Sacrifice (11—16)

Most of Mark's gospel tells the story of the Last Week. Specific details receive special attention, such as the triumphal entry into Jerusalem (ch. 11); the driving of the greedy money changers from the Temple area (ch. 11); the open hostility toward the Lord from the Pharisees and Sadducees (ch. 12); the coming judgment on Jerusalem (ch. 13); the Passover and Last Supper (ch. 14); Gethsemane (ch. 14); the betrayal, arrest, and trial (ch. 14); and finally the Crucifixion (ch. 15).

Concerning the Last Supper, it is instructive to learn that the Passover meal followed a standard pattern in Jewish homes. Prior to the meal, everyone would wash their hands. It was at this point that Jesus probably washed the feet of the disciples (John 13:4–12). The meal proper began with an opening prayer, which consisted of the blessing of the cup. This was the first of four cups of wine passed round during the ceremony. After the first cup of wine was tasted, each person would take bitter herbs and dip them in salt water (Matt. 26:23). Next, the head of the family would take one of three flat cakes of unleavened bread, break it, and put some aside. In response to a question from the youngest member of the family, the story of the first Passover would be told, and Psalms 113 and 114 would be sung.

The second cup (Luke 22:17) would be filled and passed around. Grace would be offered; the bread would be broken. Bitter herb dipped in sauce is distributed (which is when Jesus gave the sop to Judas, John 13:26). The festive meal of roast lamb is eaten. After this, Jesus instituted the Lord's Supper by breaking the bread laid aside earlier. A third cup of wine, the cup of blessing, is passed (Matt. 26:26, 28). The ritual continues with the singing of the remaining "Hallel" *(hallelujah)* Psalms (115—118) and the "Great Hallel" Psalm 136 (cp. Matt. 26:30). The final cup of wine is drunk, where Jesus said, "This is My blood of the new testament (covenant), which is shed for many" (Mark 14:24).

Chapter 16

The resurrection and the forty days prior to the ascension are dealt with in this final chapter. The general events associated with the resurrection of Christ may be summarized, keeping in mind that specific details and the exact chronology of events are not agreed upon by all Bible students (cp. Matt. 28:1–10; Mark 16:1–11; Luke 24:1–12; John 20:1–18).

The Resurrection of Jesus Christ

Late Saturday afternoon, during the early part of the evening, Mary Magdalene, Mary the mother of James, and Salome purchased some spices in preparation for the anointing of the body of Jesus. They had followed Joseph of Arimathaea to the burial site and knew exactly where the Lord was buried. Mark 16:1, "And when the Sabbath was past, Mary Magdalene, and Mary the mother of James, and Salome, had bought sweet spices, that they might come and anoint him" (cp. Matt. 28:1).

Rising early on the first day of the week, Sunday morning, Mary Magdalene, Mary the mother of James, and Salome decided to visit the tomb. Mark 16:2, "And very early in the morning the first day of the week, they came unto the sepulcher at the rising of the sun" (cp. Luke 24:1).

Mary Magdalene must have arrived first at the sepulcher, for she saw that the stone had been taken away from the grave and that the body was gone. Extremely upset, Mary Magdalene fled the area to find Simon Peter and John who, upon hearing the news, moved as quickly as they could towards the burial site. John 20:1–4, "The first day of the week cometh Mary Magdalene early, when it was yet dark, unto the sepulcher, and seeth the stone taken away from the sepulcher. Then she runneth, and cometh to Simon Peter, and to the other disciple, whom Jesus loved, and saith unto them, They have taken away the Lord out of the sepulcher, and we know not where they have laid him. Peter therefore went forth, and that other disciple, and came to the sepulcher. So they ran both together."

While Mary Magdalene went in search of Peter and John, Mary, the mother of James, and Salome arrived at the tomb along with some other women (cp. Luke 24:1,10). Later, the women would have different parts to contribute to the telling of the story. Their narrative began by remembering that on the way to the tomb, a general discussion took place as to how entrance would be gained into the sepulcher. Mark 16:3, "And they said among themselves, Who shall roll us away the stone from the door of the sepulcher?"

When the women arrived at the tomb, to everyone's amazement, the massive stone covering had been rolled away! Matthew 28:2, "And, behold, there was a great earthquake: for the angel of the Lord descended from heaven, and came and rolled back the stone from the door, and sat upon it" (cp. Mark 16:4; Luke 24:2; John 20:1).

The women who had been apprehensive about the Roman soldiers now saw that they posed no threat to anyone. Indeed, they had become living corpses. Matthew 28:4, "And for fear of him the keepers did shake, and became as dead men."

Since there was nothing to fear from the soldiers, and since the tomb was wide open, the women were inclined to go in when suddenly, they saw an angel! He was sitting on the top of the stone which he had rolled from the door of the grave. Matthew 28:2, "And, behold, there was a great earthquake: for the angel of the Lord descended from heaven, and came and rolled back the stone from the door, and sat upon it."

The appearance of the angel was spectacular. Matthew 28:3, "His countenance was like lightning, and his raiment white as snow."

The angel began to speak. Matthew 28:5–7, "And the angel answered and said unto the women, Fear not ye: for I know that ye seek Jesus, which was crucified. He is not here: for he is risen, as he said. Come, see the place where the Lord lay. And go quickly, and tell his disciples that he is risen from the dead; and, behold, he goeth before you into Galilee; there shall ye see him: lo, I have told you."

Obedient to the heavenly injunction, some of the women departed only to be met by the resurrected Lord Himself who spoke to them! Matthew 28:8–10, "And they departed quickly from the sepulcher with fear and great joy; and did run to bring his disciples word. And as they went to tell his disciples, behold, Jesus met them, saying, All hail. And they came and held him by the feet, and worshipped him. Then said Jesus unto them, Be not afraid: go tell my brethren that they go into Galilee, and there shall they see me."

While some of the women were meeting the Lord on the road leading back to Jerusalem, others stayed behind to enter into the tomb. Once inside the burial chamber, the women were amazed to discover more angelic beings. One had been sitting at the site where the Lord's body had lain. Mark 16:5, "And entering into the sepulcher, they saw a young man sitting on the right side, clothed in a long white garment; and they were affrighted . . ." The angel stood up, and another angel appeared to stand with him. Luke 24:4, "And it came to pass, as they were much perplexed thereabout, behold, two men stood by them in shining garments."

The more youthful looking angel began to speak. Mark 16:6–7, "And he saith unto them, Be not affrighted: Ye seek Jesus of Nazareth, which was crucified: he is risen; he is not here: behold the place where they laid him. But go your way, tell his disciples and Peter that he goeth before you into Galilee: there shall ye see him, as he said unto you."

Then the other angel spoke. He, too, wanted the women not to be afraid, and not to bow before them. There was good news. Luke 24:5–7 "And as they were afraid, and bowed down their faces to the earth, they said unto them, Why seek ye the living among the dead? He is not here, but is risen: remember how he spake unto you when he was yet in Galilee, Saying, The Son of man must be delivered into the hands of sinful men, and be crucified, and the third day rise again."

The women arose from their prostrate position before the angels and departed in haste to tell the eleven, and everyone else they could find, the good news about the Living Lord. Mark 16:8, "And they went out quickly, and fled from the sepulcher; for they trembled and were amazed: neither said they any thing to any man; for they were afraid." Luke 24:9, "And returned from the sepulcher, and told all these things unto the eleven, and to all the rest."

Soon after the departure of the women from the tomb, Peter and John arrived, rather breathless. They had been running, with John taking the lead over Peter. Though John was the first of the disciples to arrive at the grave, he did not want to go inside. John 20:5, "And he stooping down, and looking in, saw the linen clothes lying; yet went he not in."

Peter had no such hesitation. He who could be vacillating and fearful could also be bold as a lion. Peter was determined to see just what had happened. John 20:6–10, "Then cometh Simon Peter following him, and went into the sepulcher, and seeth the linen clothes lie. And the napkin, that was about his head, not lying with the linen clothes, but wrapped together in a place by itself. Then went in also that other disciple, which came first to the sepulcher, and he saw, and believed. For as yet they knew not the scripture, that he must rise again from the dead. Then the disciples went away again unto their own home."

Now Mary Magdalene, who had finally caught up with Peter and John, stayed behind after their departure. It did not matter if the men left because during this period, no one was really talking much. They were all too amazed at the situation. Besides, no one knew for certain what was happening. John and Peter did not perceive that Jesus had arisen from the dead, nor did Mary. She thought that someone had stolen the body, or at least moved it. All Mary could do for the moment was to stand and weep and wonder. John 20:11, "But Mary stood without at the sepulcher weeping: and as she wept, she stooped down, and looked into the sepulcher."

With the teardrops still streaming down her face, Mary looked inside the sepulcher. Though she did not know it, Mary was looking into the face of heavenly creatures, for the angels were now back. John did not see them. Peter did not see them, but Mary did. John 20:12, "And seeth two angels in white sitting, the one at the head, and the other at the feet, where the body of Jesus had lain."

One of the angels began to speak. John 20:13a, "And they say unto her, Woman, why weepest thou?" Mary responded in John 20:13b. "She saith unto them, Because they have taken away my Lord, and I know not where they have laid him."

That was all she could say. Standing up from her stooped position, Mary began to weep again. Though sobbing heavily, she heard another voice. Mary turned towards the voice. John 20:14a, "And when she had thus said, she turned herself back, and saw Jesus standing . . . ."

But she did not know it was the Lord. John 20:14b, ". . . and knew not that it was Jesus."

Oh, but in matchless and marvelous grace, the Lord began to speak to this lady who loved Him so much. John 20:15a, "Jesus saith unto her, Woman, why weepest thou? whom seekest thou?" Mary, thinking that she was speaking to a gardener said unto Him, John 20:15b, "Sir, if thou have borne him hence, tell me where thou hast laid him, and I will take him away." How Mary thought she might move the body without the help of anyone else is not known. Love has a strength of its own. But no, Mary, you do not have to take the body anywhere. And Mary, you are not talking to a gardener. You are talking to your God!

John 20:16, "Jesus saith unto her, Mary." Just one word—that was all Jesus said, and it was enough. Her name, and her Lord. It was the Lord! Jesus once said, "My sheep hear my voice. They know it and they follow me." Mary Magdalene knew the voice of her Shepherd. With sudden force Mary turned herself in the direction of the Voice, John 20:16b, "and saith unto him, 'Rabboni;' which is to say, 'Master!'" Yes, Mary, it is the Master. Rushing to Him, Mary Magdalene embraced her Lord and her Savior with all the love that a surprised and joyous heart can express. So fierce was her grasp on the Lord that something had to be said. John

20:17a, "Jesus saith unto her, Touch me not; for I am not yet ascended to my Father."

Jesus had something He wanted Mary to do. She must go and share what she had seen. She must tell the men. So Jesus said to Mary, John 20:17b, ". . . go to my brethren, and say unto them, I ascend unto my Father, and your Father; and to my God, and your God."

In obedience to the will of the Lord, Mary went. John 20:18, "Mary Magdalene came and told the disciples that she had seen the Lord, and that he had spoken these things unto her."

Fourteen Glorious Appearances of the Risen Christ

1.	To Mary Magdalene	Mark 16:9–10
2.	To the other women	Matthew 28:9–10
3.	To those on the Emmaus Road	Mark 16:12–13
4.	To Peter	Luke 24:34
5.	To the Eleven (except Thomas)	Luke 24:36–45
6.	To the Eleven (Thomas present)	John 20:24–31
7.	To the Seven at the Sea of Galilee	John 21
8.	To the Eleven and 500 in Galilee	Matthew 28:16–20; 1 Corinthians 15:6
9.	To James	1 Corinthians 15:7
10.	To the Eleven	Acts 1:3
11.	To Saul of Tarsus	Acts 9:3–6
12.	To Stephen	Acts 7:55
13.	To Paul in the Temple	Acts 22:17–21; 23:11
14.	To John on the Isle of Patmos	Revelation 1:10–19

6

The Perfect Man

THE GOSPEL ACCORDING TO LUKE

Written c. A.D. 60
Key word: "Perfect Man"

"For the Son of Man is come to seek and to save that which was lost."

—Luke 19:10

Why Written: Presenting Christ as Perfect Man

Whereas *Mark* presents the life of Jesus in snapshots which cascade one after another into our minds, *Luke* flows like a deep river. Luke is concerned with the humanity of Christ, as well as His deity. Only in *Luke* do we have the peasant parents at His birth, His growth as a boy, and the human pressure He felt at Gethsemane.

And Luke is presenting Christ to the Greek mind. Remember, although Rome had conquered the Greeks and the world, the Romans and the world were conquered *culturally* by the Greek mind-set. The Greek philosophies and way of thinking were pervasive throughout the Roman Empire. The Greek mind had a craving for perfection and high achievement. They sought to create a *perfect man:* with knowledge about all things, with flawless physical body, with emotions under control and ruled by reason. The Greek mind-set wanted a rational explanation for all things.

So Luke explains the Jewish culture when necessary for the Greek understanding. And he presents Jesus: a peasant without a formal education, yet with super-human intellect and physical powers. Jesus was not a cross between the two extremes, but a perfect "fullness" of humanity and deity.

The Life of Luke

The third gospel was written by Luke, the only known non-Jewish writer in the Bible. Because his name is mentioned three times in the New Testament, several things are known about him. First, Luke was a close friend of the Apostle Paul (Phil. 1:24; 2 Tim. 4:11). Second, he was a man of culture and education. In Colossians 4:14 he is referred to as "Luke the beloved physician." Third, Luke was a conscientious historian and author. His faithfulness to known facts have amazed modern archeologists and given external validity to the inspiration of the Bible. Sir William Ramsay spent many years of his life in intensive archaeological research in Asia Minor. It was his testimony that, "Luke's history is unsurpassed in respect to its trustworthiness" (*The Bearing of Recent Discovery on the Trustworthiness of the New Testament*).

Tradition says that Luke first became a Christian at Antioch, in Syria, where the gospel arrived prior to the great missionary efforts of Peter or Paul, Barnabas or John Mark (note Acts 11:19–21). As a Christian, Luke found a faithful friend in Paul, and traveled with him through part of the apostle's Second Missionary Journey (Acts 16:10–15). It is probable that Luke did not complete the Second Journey, but remained at Philippi to continue the work of the ministry.

Six years later, when Paul was on his Third Missionary Journey, Luke re-united with him on his way to Jerusalem. It was a dangerous period in Paul's life, for he had made many Jewish enemies. A plan had been formulated by these enemies to murder Paul. Though an attempt was made on his life, in the providence of the Lord Roman guards came to Paul's rescue. In the middle of the night he was taken to Caesarea, the Roman capital of Judea, where he was presented to Felix, the governor of the district of Judea. Luke was an eyewitness to all of these events.

Felix ordered that Paul be kept in Herod's palace with freedom of movement. For two years Paul lived under "house arrest." While the apostle was in custody, Luke was free to come and go as he pleased, for no charges had been brought against him. The evidence suggests that Luke used this time to collect data, visit with those who had known the Lord Jesus Christ, and fellowship with new believers. There were many devout Christians in Caesarea, including Philip and his four daughters. And there were many Christians elsewhere, such as Mary (the mother of Jesus), who lived with the Apostle John (possibly her nephew) in Jerusalem. From Mary, and also from Elizabeth, Luke would learn the details of their personal conversations, the visit by the angel Gabriel, and of the lovely songs they composed. The songs of these two great ladies of grace have inspired non-canonical musical masterpieces, such as *Ave Maria*, the *Benedictus*, the *Magnificat*, and the *Gloria in Excelsis*. Perhaps Luke also went to Bethlehem, only five miles south of Jerusalem, and spoke to the innkeeper, and maybe some shepherds. He was determined to speak to eye-witnesses.

Meanwhile, Paul's enemies in Jerusalem continued to try to kill him, and Felix was replaced as governor by Porcius Festus. Finally, frustrated with his ordeal, the apostle decided to make a personal appeal to Caesar to hear his case. This was his legal right as a Roman citizen. Paul's appeal to Caesar was granted and he was finally placed on board a boat to cross the Mediterranean. It was a violent voyage (Acts 27—28) but, in the spring of A.D. 61, Paul arrived in Rome together with Luke. It was decided that the apostle would be kept in the custody of a Roman soldier, but that he could rent his own house and receive his own friends.

The next part of the life of Paul is a little obscure, but it is possible that Paul was tried in Rome, acquitted of the charges against him, and released c. A.D. 63/64. He returned to his missionary work throughout Greece and Asia Minor only to be re-charged by his enemies in Jerusalem and re-arrested. During this second imprisonment, Luke was Paul's only companion (2 Tim. 4:11). It is a tragic thought to think of the great apostle as virtually alone at the last (2 Tim. 1:15). He who was a source of blessing to so many others was left by himself to suffer the death of a martyr by beheading.

The end of the life of Luke is not known. There is an ancient legend which says that Luke spent his final years as an evangelist in Bithynia, a province to the north of Asia Minor, where he died at age 74.

Overview of Luke

The *Gospel* by Luke may be grouped into three sections:

Section	Chapters
Perfect Birth	1—4:13, *Birth, John the Baptist, Temptation*
Perfect Life	4:14—19:28, *Preaching, Teaching, Miracles*
Perfect Death	19:29—24, *The Last Week*

Perfect Birth (1—4:13)

Chapter 1:1-4

The preface of the book provided by Luke explains to his friend Theophilus the purpose for his writing. Though *many* accounts were beginning to circulate concerning the events associated with the life of Christ, Luke was determined to set forth in an *orderly* manner an *accurate* account based upon apostolic memories and eye-witness testimonies—all guided by the Holy Spirit.

Chapters 1:5—2:52

The birth of Christ is described in great detail, which includes the annunciation to Zacharias, Mary, and Elizabeth, the birth of John the Baptist, the conversations between Mary and Elizabeth, and their splendid songs of praise. Throughout the life of Christ, angels would have a pervasive presence. An angel announced the birth of His forerunner (Luke 1:11–17), and named him (1:13). An angel appeared to Mary to tell of the birth of the Messiah (1:26–37), and also to Joseph (Matt. 1:20–21). A group of angels manifested themselves to the shepherds that the Great Shepherd had been born (Luke 2:8–15), and sang songs to their Sovereign (Luke 2:13–14). An angel warned Joseph to flee to Egypt (Matt. 2:13, 20). The years passed and the Lord reached maturity. Still, He would need heavenly under-girding—and so we find that angels ministered to Him at His baptism (John 1:51), following His temptation (Matt. 4:11), and while He prayed in Gethsemane (Luke 22:43). Twelve legions of angels were ready to deliver Him from death if He wanted to summon them (Matt. 26:53). Finally, the angels came to the Lord's burial site to roll the stone away, and to let the world know that He was alive (Matt. 28:2, 5–7; John 20:11–14).

While the public ministry of Christ is filled with the miraculous, most of His childhood, from age 12 to 30, appears to be very normal. The Father has drawn a curtain of silence across these 18 years.

Chapters 3:1—4:13 (John the Baptist)

The narrative continues with preparation for public ministry via the work of John the Baptist, the baptism of Christ, the Lord's legal right to the claim of Messiah, and His victory over temptation. Following His triumph over the devil, the Lord would have many things to say about Satan during His ministry. Satan is called "the enemy" (Matt. 13:39), the "evil one" (Matt. 13:38), the "prince of this world" (John 12:31; 4:30), a "liar" (John 8:44), and "a murderer" (John 8:44). Let no one doubt that we face a real and personal enemy in the devil.

Perfect Life (4:14—19:28)

Chapters 4:14—9:50 (The Greater Galilean Ministry)

After teaching and healing many people in various parts of Galilee, Jesus returned to His boyhood home, Nazareth. Going into the local synagogue on the Sabbath day, the Lord selected a text from the prophet Isaiah (Isa. 61:1–2a) as part of a public proclamation of His message and ministry:

> The Spirit of the Lord is upon Me, because He has anointed Me to preach the gospel to the poor; He hath sent Me to heal the brokenhearted, to preach deliverance to the captives, and recovering of sight to the blind; to set at liberty them that are bruised, to preach the acceptable year of the Lord (Luke 4:18–19).

This is a significant moment in two ways. First, everyone understood this text as a prophecy of the Messiah. Jesus was declaring Himself to be their Messiah when in the next verses He said, "This day is this Scripture fulfilled in your ears!" (Luke 4:21). Second, Jesus here unfolds something that the Jews had failed to understand: the Messiah would come two times, not once. The first coming would be as a Servant (Isa. 61:1–2a). Notice this in Jesus' careful ending of the reading in the middle of verse 2. Only the words to that point were "fulfilled in your ears" that day in Nazareth. The remainder of verse two says "and the day of vengeance of our God." This is a reference to the Day of the Lord, the second coming of Christ in judgment upon the earth, still to be fulfilled at a later time.

The Nazarenes had a choice at that moment, as does every human being since then: we must either take Jesus at His word that He is the Messiah, and worship Him, or we must reject Him as a false teacher and blasphemer. (To accept Him as only a "good teacher" is not an option which He offered.) Their disastrous and condemning choice is a matter of the public record in Luke 4:28ff.

When He was rejected by the people of Nazareth, the Lord departed for Capernaum on the Sea of Galilee where he would spend the next two years. His ministry would expand "into every place of the country round about" (Luke 4:37). On occasion the Lord even went to Tyre and Sidon, explaining, "I must preach the kingdom of God to other cities also; for therefore am I sent" (Luke 4:43). Luke records the message of the Lord known as the Sermon on the Mount (Luke 6:20–49) with the Golden Rule (Luke 6:31).

As Luke records the preaching and teaching of the Lord, he is careful to provide the particular reason which prompted each message and miracle. Luke is also mindful to share three prayers of Christ on three specific occasions. There is prayer after the cleansing of a leper (5:16), before the calling of the Twelve Apostles (6:12), and at His Transfiguration (9:29).

Chapters 9:51—19:27 (The Perean Ministry)

From Galilee, Jesus ministered on the east side of the Jordan River, in the district of Perea, with special trips into Jerusalem. This period took place about six months before the Passion Week, from the fall of A.D. 29 to the spring of A.D. 30. During this time the Lord told many wonderful parables, including the Good Samaritan, the Prodigal Son, and the Rich Man and Lazarus.

In Luke 16 the Lord spoke about the sufferings of the unrighteous in their place of hell. Technically, "hell" (Gk. *hades*, Heb. *sheol*) is the place where all the physically dead went according to Old Testament biblical theology. The righteous dead went to one sphere of this place of the spirit world, referred to as *Abraham's bosom* (Luke 16:29). They were separated from the wicked dead by a *great gulf* (Luke 16:26). [Note: The believing thief went to *Paradise* (Luke 23:43), while Paul spoke of the *Third Heaven* (2 Cor. 12:1–4) being in the presence of the Lord (study 1 Cor. 15:53; 1 Thess. 4:13–18; 2 Cor. 5:2; Phil. 1:23).]

During the months of the Perean Ministry, Jesus sent forth the Seventy. He taught about the two greatest commandments, the definition of a neighbor, instruction in prayer, the prophecy of the coming judgment upon national Israel, teachings on the nature of the kingdom of God, and finally, the predictions of His impending death.

Perfect Death (19:29—24)

Chapters 19:29—23 (The Last Week)

Luke faithfully records the Triumphal Entry into Jerusalem, the final teachings of Christ in the Temple, the Last Supper, the discourse to the disciples on the Mount of Olives, His betrayal, arrest, six trials, violent crucifixion, and burial.

Chapter 24 (The Resurrection and the Ascension)

Three appearances of Christ are made to His disciples. On the road to Emmaus, two disciples hear the Lord's personal interpretation of the Scriptures beginning with Moses and the prophets. (The same personal instruction is available to us, as we read His Word illumined by the Holy Spirit - our hearts should burn within us!) His last instructions are given to those who will be witnesses for Him unto the ends of the earth.

A Traditional Diary of the Last Week

Palm Sunday
Jesus rode into Jerusalem　　　　　　　　Mark 11:1–11
　　Spent the night at Bethany

Monday
Cleansing of the Temple　　　　　　　　Mark 11:15–19
　　Spent the night at Bethany

Tuesday

Teaching in the Temple	Luke 20–21
The challenge to authority	Luke 20:1–8
Parable of the Husbandman	Luke 20:9–18
The question of paying tribute	Luke 20:19–26
The question of resurrection	Luke 20:27–41
The question of David's son	Luke 20:40–44
Warning against the scribes	Luke 20:45–47
The widow's mite	Luke 21:1–4
The coming judgment on Israel	Luke 21:5–28
	Matt. 24–25
The parables of: the Fig Tree,	Luke 21:29–36
The Talents, The Foolish Virgins	
Mary anoints Jesus at Bethany	John 12:2–8
Spent the night at Bethany	

Wednesday

The Great Conspiracy	Matt 26:1–16
	Luke 22:3–6
Spent the night at Bethany	Luke 22:1–6

Thursday

The Last Supper	Matt 25:17–20
	John 13:1–30
	Mark 14:22–26
The protest of Peter	Luke 22:7–30
The washing of the disciples' feet	Matt 26:36–56
	Luke 22:39–53
The prayer in Gethsemane	John 17

Good Friday

The Betrayal and Arrest	Mark 14:43–50

	John 28:1–12
Jesus before Annas	John 18:12–24
Jesus before Caiaphas	Mark 14:53–65
Peter's Tragic Denial	Matt 26:69–75
	John 18:15–27
Jesus before Sanhedrin	Luke 22:66–71
Judas commits suicide	Matt 27:3–10
Jesus before Pilate	Mark 14:66–72
	Luke 23:1–5
Jesus before Herod Antipas	Luke 23:6–12
Sentenced by Pilate	Luke 23:13–25
The Crucifixion	Matt 27:1–61
1. Arrival at Golgotha	Mark 15:22
2. Offered gall	Matt 27:34
3. The impaling	Matt 27:35
4. The first cry	Luke 23:34

    "Father, forgive them; for they know not what they do."

5. Gambling for garments	Matt 27:35
6. Jesus ridiculed	Mark 15:29
7. Salvation of a thief	Matt 27:44
8. The second cry	Luke 23:43

    "Today shalt thou be with Me in paradise."

9. The third cry	John 19:26–27

    "Woman, behold thy Son! Behold thy mother!"

10. The fourth cry	Mark 15:34-36, Matt. 27:46

    "My God, My God, why hast Thou forsaken Me?"

11. The fifth cry	John 19:28

    "I thirst."

12. The sixth cry	John 19:30

    "It is finished."

13. The seventh cry   Luke 23:46
  "Father, into Thy hands I commend My spirit."
14. Jesus dismisses His spirit   Mark 15:37

The burial of Jesus   Luke 23:1–56
                                           John 19:31–42
                                           Matt 27:62–66
                                           Mark 15:46

AND ON THE THIRD DAY, HE ROSE AGAIN!

Map of Jerusalem during the Last Week

1. *The Upper Room.* Site of the Last Supper the night before the crucifixion.
2. *House of Caiaphas.* High priest, presided at trial before the Sanhedrin.
3. *Praetorium.* Roman governor's headquarters; Jesus was tried before Pilate.
4. *House of Herod Antipas.* Ruler of Galilee and Perea during Jesus' ministry. He mocked Christ before returning him to Pilate for trial (Matt. 14:1–11).
5. *Golgotha* ("the skull"). The place where Jesus Christ was crucified. It lay outside the city walls of Jerusalem in NT times, and was visible from some distance. Little evidence exists to verify the exact location.
6. *Tomb of Jesus.* The rock tomb, sealed with a large rolled stone, close to the place of crucifixion. Early reports lend support to this traditional site.
7. *Herod's Palace.* Administrative center, treasury, and royal home.

7

The Son of God

THE GOSPEL ACCORDING TO JOHN

Written: early date, prior to A.D. 70; late date, c. A.D. 90
Key phrase: "Son of God"

"But these are written, that ye might believe that Jesus is the Christ, the Son of God; and that believing ye might have life through his name."

—John 20:31

Why Written: Presenting Christ as the Son of God

The three synoptic Gospels have much in common, but John confronts us with 92% new information. The four gospels fit together in a profound and beautiful way to form a timeless evangelistic sermon with four key points: (1) Jesus is the Messiah; (2) Jesus is the perfect servant; (3) Jesus is the perfect man (in His wisdom and compassion); and now (4) John's Gospel makes a final appeal, the great application: "What will you do with Jesus?" While the three present the facts, John challenges us to apply the facts: "Will you come to Him?" This is evidenced by the personal encounters with Nicodemus (ch. 3), the woman at the well (ch. 4), and the crippled man at the Pool of Bethesda (ch. 5).

Galilee is the primary setting for the Synoptics; *John* takes place mostly in Jerusalem, where the teaching of Jesus is in stark contrast to the religious leaders. Jesus clearly presents Himself as 'one with the Father'—God incarnate. Each of us is forced to make a clear choice: "is Jesus the Deity as He claims to be, or not?" There is no middle ground to accept Him as a 'good teacher' and nothing more. He is either a liar to be rejected, or God to be worshiped and bowed to as Lord of our lives.

John emphasized the deity of Christ as the Son of God. His Gospel contains eight "I Am" statements of the Lord, which reflect God's own name of self-existence: YHWH, or Jehovah, translated "I AM" in Exodus 3:14.

I Am the Bread of Life	John 6:35, 38
I Am the Light of the World	John 8:12; 9:5
I Am . . . before Abraham	John 8:58
I Am the Door	John 10:7, 9
I Am the Good Shepherd	John 10:11–14
I Am the Resurrection and the Life	John 11:25
I Am the Way, the Truth, the Life	John 14:6
I Am the Vine	John 15:4

The Disciple Whom Jesus Loved

John is one of the most important figures of the New Testament, and one of the most prolific writers of Scripture. Five of the New Testament books are the product of his pen: the *Gospel of John, 1 John, 2 John, 3 John*, and the book of *The Revelation*. John and his brother James were the sons of Zebedee and Salome, who may have been a sister of Mary, the mother of Jesus (Matt. 27:56; Mark 15:40, cp. John 19:25). If that is true, then John, about the same age as Jesus, knew the Lord in childhood as a cousin—and in manhood as Christ, the Messiah.

John is introduced initially by the other Gospel writers (Matthew, Mark, and Luke) as part of a successful family fishing business which was able to employ hired servants. He lived at Capernaum on the northwest shore of the Sea of Galilee, had a house in Jerusalem (John 19:27), and enjoyed personal acquaintance with the high-priest (John 18:15-16). However, in his own *Gospel* we meet John and Andrew as disciples of John the Baptist (John 1:35, 40), who was preaching and baptizing on the east side of the Jordan in the area of Bethany.

One day, Jesus appeared as John was ministering. The Baptist recognized Jesus as the Messiah, and called the attention of John and Andrew to that fact. It was about ten o'clock in the morning when the two fishermen made a fundamental decision to forsake all and follow the Lord. The rest of the day and the evening were spent with Jesus. Andrew was anxious for the dawning of a new morning. He wanted to go and find his brother Simon and bring him to Jesus. When Jesus met Simon, He said unto him, "'Thou art Simon, the son of Jonah: thou shalt be called Cephas,' which is by interpretation, a 'stone'" (John 1:42). From that day forward, Peter would never be too far from the Lord, and neither would John.

The day following Peter's introduction to Christ, Jesus moved from the east side of the Jordan opposite Judah, and went to Galilee (John 1:43), where Philip was found together with his friend Nathanael (also known as Bartholomew). Nathanael lived at Cana of Galilee where a wedding was about to be held. Jesus and His disciples were invited to the celebration. A social concern arose at the wedding which the Lord met by graciously and miraculously turning the water into wine. By this display of sovereign power, the hearts of the Lord's new disciples were turned so that they believed in Him (John 2:11).

There would be many other miracles which John would be privileged to witness as he worked with Jesus for the next three and one half years. John, with Peter and James, would be those closest to the Lord. Perhaps the Lord realized that James and John in particular needed personal attention, for they had violent tempers (cp. Mark 3:17). Jesus allowed John to be present at the resurrection of the daughter of Jarius, at the

Transfiguration, and in the hour of agony in the Garden of Gethsemane. At the Last Supper, it was John who was given the place of honor at the right hand of the Lord (John 13:23). His mother had once sought for John and his brother *the* greatest place of honor in the kingdom of heaven. While that request was denied as being too presumptuous, in private and according to Divine prerogative, John was given a place of honor (cp. Matt. 20:21).

John's Journey

At the end of the Lord's public ministry, John followed at a discreet distance as soldiers took the Lord from Gethsemane into the place of the high priest, to Pilate's praetorium (place of judgment), and then to Golgotha. John stood beneath the Cross on which Christ suffered, and stayed there until He died. Three days later, when the report came that the tomb in which Jesus was buried was empty, John was among the first to race to the burial site to see what that meant (John 20:1–10). A few hours later he knew what it meant, for he saw the resurrected Lord (John 20:19–38).

After the Ascension of Christ, John was with the other disciples when the power of the Holy Spirit came at Pentecost. Following that monumental day, Peter and John remained in Jerusalem to advance the gospel of the kingdom of heaven. John was still in Jerusalem when the Apostle Paul returned from his First Missionary Journey (c. A.D. 50), and so John was able to take part in The Great Jerusalem Council (Acts 15, cp. Gal. 2:9).

In later years, it would be said that John ministered in Ephesus, and suffered for the sake of the gospel he preached. He suffered spiritual persecution because he combated the heresy of the *Gnostics*, who denied that Jesus was come in the flesh (1 John). The Gnostics, literally *"the knowing ones,"* tried to find a solution to the question of how physical man can have fellowship with a God who is spirit. How are matter and spirit related? How did evil come into existence? The Gnostics thought they had discovered a solution to these questions. They believed that emancipation from the body came through knowledge (Gk. *gnosis*). At this point the Gnostics divided into two major schools of thought. Those who followed Cerinthus believed that Jesus was both good and evil; He was both flesh and Spirit. In contrast, the *Docetists* denied the fleshly or "evil" nature of Jesus, and taught that Jesus had no real human nature but only a spiritual one. Together, the teaching of the Gnostics denied the true Incarnation of Jesus: that He was true humanity but free of sin. There were other problems which John had to combat on behalf of the Church, such as immorality. Though an "Apostle of Love," John was not hesitant to correct doctrinal and moral error.

In addition to the spiritual battles he fought, John suffered religious and political persecution under Domitian (A.D. 51–96; ruler of Rome, A.D. 81–96). Irenaeus (c. 175–195, bishop of Lyons in southern France) states that the Apostle John continued to live at Ephesus after being freed by Nerva (A.D. 35–98; emperor, A.D. 96–98, Domitian's successor), and that he died in the reign of Trajan (A.D. 98–117). If Irenaeus is correct, John would have been over one hundred years of age. The "disciple whom Jesus loved" (cp. John 13:23; 19:26; 20:2; 21:7, 20) went to the One whom he loved.

Overview of John

John's Gospel can be grouped into three sections:

Section	Chapters
Deity Proclaimed	1—12, *Preaching, Teaching, Miracles*
Deity Explained	13—17, *The Last Supper and prayer*
Deity Defamed	18—21, *The last week*

Deity Proclaimed (1—12)

Chapter 1:1–18 (The Deity of Christ)

The deity of Jesus Christ is clearly revealed in this wonderful introduction, whereby John declares that he beheld the glory of the Lord, the Light of the World. Time and again Jesus will be presented in this manner (cp. John 8:12; 9:5; 12:46 with 1 John 1:5–7). It was the apostle's desire that all men might believe on Christ and have eternal life.

Chapter 1:19–34

In the Gospels written by Matthew, Mark, and Luke, the writers pass directly from the time of temptation by Satan to the Galilean Ministry (Matt. 4:11–12; Mark 1:13–14; Luke 4:13–14). John takes the reader back to the period when Jesus returned from the wilderness before departing for Galilee. John the Baptist testifies that Jesus is the Messiah and the Son of God. Though the Baptizer had known Jesus since childhood, he did not know that Jesus was the Messiah until he saw the Holy Spirit descending and remaining on Him (note 1:33). "And I saw, and bare record that this is the Son of God" (cp. 1:34). When a committee of Jews from Jerusalem was sent by the Sanhedrin to question John, to discover if he were the Christ or Elijah, John humbly declared that he was simply "the voice of one crying in the wilderness, Make straight the way of the Lord, as said the prophet Esaias" (1:23).

Chapter 1:35–51

As the Lord began His public ministry, He called unto Himself the first five of twelve disciples. There were Andrew and John, Simon and Philip, and Nathanael. Nathanael was initially a skeptic when told that He had been found, "of whom Moses in the law, and the prophets, did write, Jesus of Nazareth, the son of Joseph" (1:45). The last word Nathanael heard was, "Nazareth," and he did not have a high opinion of people from that community. In sarcastic honesty he asked, "Can there any good thing come out of Nazareth?" (1:46). Rather than argue, Philip wisely said, "Come and see." Nathanael came and he saw the Savior, and was convinced by the Majesty of Christ (1:49). Let each seeker of Truth respond to this simple invitation: "Come and see."

Chapters 2—4

In these chapters John sets forth the ministry of Christ in a series of miracles, messages, and mighty words.

Miracles as Proof. John records seven 'sign' miracles overall, which serve as a framework for his narrative up to the last Passover, and are proof of the deity which Christ everywhere displayed.

(1) Water to wine	2:1
(2) Nobleman's son	4:46
(3) Pool of Bethesda	5:1
(4) 5,000 fed	6:1
(5) Walking on water	6:15
(6) Man born blind	9:1
(7) Lazarus	11:1

Personal Interviews. This section also records the two very important personal interviews: the intimate one-on-one encounters with Nicodemus (ch. 3) and with the woman at the well (ch. 4). In these, individuals like each one of us meet the Living God face to face, and are challenged with the reality of relationship with Him as the life-changing Lord.

Of particular interest is the first miracle in Cana of Galilee, located about four miles northeast of Nazareth, and the first cleansing of the Temple (Chapter 2). The changing of water into wine amazed the servants as well as the disciples, for the six waterpots contained "two or three firkins apiece" (2:6) (between 16 and 24 gallons), for a total of 96 to 126 gallons of fresh wine. It was a miracle of great abundance. In chapter 3 Nicodemus is told that he must be *"born again."* When Nicodemus confesses his ignorance of the meaning of the new spiritual birth, the Lord explains to him in simple language that salvation is a sovereign act of God, made effective by the secret work of the Holy Spirit (3:8). Before the night was over, Nicodemus understood what constitutes a biblical Christian.[1]

Following his conversation with Nicodemus, the Lord and His disciples went into the land of Judea, where John the Baptist continued to speak of Christ (3:22–36). Moving into Chapter 4, the story is told of how Jesus gave to the woman of Samaria the spiritual water of life, while sitting on a well which was itself literally 100 feet deep and 9 feet in diameter.

Chapters 5—10

In chapters 5—10, Christ performed specific miracles, including the raising of Lazarus. He offers Himself as the Bread of Life (ch. 6), the Light of the World (ch. 8), and the Good Shepherd (ch. 10). The "feast of the Jews" in Chapter 5 is not defined. There were several feasts which the Jews observed at this time, and which Christ Himself kept. *Passover* took place in April and commemorated the Exodus 1,400 years earlier. The *Feast of Pentecost* took place in June, 50 days after Passover and commemorating the giving of the Law. The *Feast of Tabernacles* was held in October, celebrating the in-gathering of harvests. The *Feast of*

---

[1] *A Biblical Christian.* Albert N. Martin has crystallized the simplicity of the gospel in Christ Jesus by stating in summary form that a biblical Christian is a person who has done four things.

First, according to the Bible, a Christian is a person who has faced realistically the problem of his own personal sin (1 Cor. 15:22; Rom. 3:10, 23). *Second*, a biblical Christian is one who has seriously considered the one divine remedy for sin, Jesus Christ (John 3:16; 1 John 4:10; Eph. 2:4). *Third*, a biblical Christian is one who has wholeheartedly complied with the terms for obtaining God's provision for sin (John 1:12). *Fourth*, a biblical Christian is a person who manifests in his life that his claims to repentance and faith are real (John 14:21–24). [See *What Is a Biblical Christian* by Albert N. Martin, available from Chapel Library.]

Dedication was the joyous remembrance in December of the revolt started by Judas Maccabaeus. Finally, there was *Purim*, observed shortly before Passover (in April) to remind the Jews of their glorious deliverance from destruction during the days of the Persians (study *Esther*). Purim is never referred to in the Gospels.

While the "feast of the Jews" in Chapter 5 is not defined, in Chapter 7 the Feast of Tabernacles (October) is in view (7:2). It had been a year and a half since Jesus was in Jerusalem. In six more months He would die there. On His prior visit to the Holy City, Jesus had healed a man on the Sabbath, and announced that He was the Son of God (5:18). The Lord knew that in their anger, the Jews planned to murder Him, and He plainly said so (7:19–23). But it was not His time to die. When the rulers sent officers to arrest the Lord, they could not do it (7:44). Following the Feast of Tabernacles, Jesus observed the Feast of Dedication two months later (10:22–39), which was held in December.

Chapter 11

About a month before His own death, Jesus performed a miracle which was used by the Sanhedrin for the main pretext as to why they should seek to put Him to death (11:48–53). Jesus raised Lazarus from the dead. This was the Lord's third act of restoring someone to life (Mark 5:21–43, Luke 7:11–17).

Chapter 12

The events of the Last Week begin to be detailed in this section. On the night prior to His great entry into Jerusalem, a supper was held at Bethany. Mary and Martha were there, as was Lazarus. Sometime during the supper, Mary took "a pound of ointment of spikenard, very costly, and anointed the feet of Jesus, and wiped his feet with her hair: and the house was filled with the odor of the ointment" (12:3). She knew that Jesus was going forth to die, and anointed Him (for burial). Following His Triumphal Entry into Jerusalem (12:9–19), certain Greeks were allowed to meet Christ, indicating the universal appeal of the gospel (12:20–36). As the gospel would be for all men without distinction, so the gospel would be victorious over Satan (see 12:27–36). And yet, the Jews as a nation would not believe on Jesus. John tells why: it was the fulfillment of Scripture (12:37–50).

Deity Explained (13—17)

In these chapters, the Lord gave His final message to the Twelve during the Last Supper. The Lord's teaching on Heaven in John 14 has been of particular comfort to the Church for centuries, as well as the promise of the Holy Spirit. Although Jesus was about to leave them physically, He was not leaving them at all, because He would send "the Comforter." The Holy Spirit indwells the true believer, and fulfills very specifically for them today the same role which Jesus served in His physical presence with His disciples: to guide, to teach, to provide, and to protect them.

The essential unity between Christ and His people is revealed in Chapter 15. In Chapter 16 the Lord warns that His followers should not be offended when they suffer for righteousness' sake. Finally, the Lord prayed for His own in the High Priestly Prayer (John 17). Following the Last Supper, Jesus went with the Apostles to Gethsemane, prior to His arrest by the Roman garrison (500–600 men). Chapters 14—17 constitute one of the wonderful high points in the New Testament, and deserve the special appropriation and understanding of every Christian.

Deity Defamed (18—21)

The illegal trials and Crucifixion of Christ are described along with the glorious Resurrection, the final moments with the Apostles, and His Ascension at Bethany (cp. Luke 24:44–51). The tender grace shown to Peter deserves special consideration (20:9–19). Three times Peter had denied the Lord, three times he would be asked the extent of his love for Christ. Three times Peter would affirm his love but not in boldness as before. Peter was no longer fleshly. He was a man sustained by the Holy Spirit, reflected in the fact that he died a martyr for the Master—just as Jesus knew he would (21:18–19).

8

Witness to the World

THE ACTS OF THE APOSTLES

Written A.D. 63
Key word: "Witnesses"

"But ye shall receive power, after that the Holy Ghost is come upon you: and ye shall be witnesses unto Me both in Jerusalem, and in all Judaea, and in Samaria, and unto the uttermost part of the earth."

—Acts 1:8

Introduction

Dr. A. T. Pierson often called the fifth book of the New Testament, *The Acts of the Holy Spirit.* There is wisdom in that descriptive title, for the Holy Spirit did guide the growth and advancement of the Church of Jesus Christ in a marvelous and miraculous way. The *Book of Acts* is filled with the mystery and majesty of a Divine movement. God the Father had promised through the prophet Joel that His Spirit would be poured out upon all flesh, so that sons and daughters would prophesy, young men would see visions, and old men would dream dreams (Acts 2:17, cp. Joel 2:28–30). The *Book of Acts* records that this actually happened.

Young men saw visions. Saul of Tarsus had a vision of the resurrected Christ (Acts 9:3–9). Ananias had a vision instructing him to minister to

Saul in Damascus (Acts 9:10–16). The Gentile Cornelius had a vision instructing him to ask Peter to come to Joppa with the gospel (Acts 10:3–6). Peter had a vision to eat unclean animals which meant to go and fellowship with the "unclean" Gentiles (Acts 10:9–18, 28). Saul, changed into the Apostle Paul, had a vision to go to Macedonia to preach the gospel (Acts 16:9). Paul had another vision that God would save souls in the wicked city of Corinth (Acts 18:9–10). He also had a vision promising the Lord's presence during his final voyage to Rome (Acts 23:11).

As the young men saw visions, so the *voice of prophecy* could be heard in the *Book of Acts*. There are several selected sermons in *Acts* which have been recorded for consideration. Peter, Paul, Stephen, and James contributed some of the most important majestic messages.

Speaking Forth the Word of Truth

Peter preached at Pentecost	Acts 2:14–40
Peter preached in the Temple	Acts 3:12–26
Peter preached to the Sanhedrin	Acts 4:5–12
Stephen preached to the Sanhedrin	Acts 7
Peter preached to the Gentiles	Acts 10:28–47
Peter spoke to the Church	Acts 11:4–18
Paul preached in Antioch	Acts 13:16–41
Peter spoke to the Jerusalem Council	Acts 15:7–11
James spoke to the Jerusalem Council	Acts 15:13–21
Paul spoke to the Ephesians	Acts 20:17–35
Paul spoke to the crowd in Jerusalem	Acts 22:1–21
Paul spoke to the Sanhedrin	Acts 23:1–6
Paul spoke before King Agrippa	Acts 26
Paul spoke to the Jewish rulers in Rome	Acts 28:17–20

Then there were *"signs and wonders"* (Acts 2:43; 5:12; 6:8; 8:6–7, 13; 14:3–4). The *Book of Acts* is filled with many marvelous miracles as Joel had predicted. Peter healed a man lame from birth at the Temple Gate (3:7–11, cp. 4:16–17). His very shadow brought recovery to the sick (5:15–16). Peter was able to raise Tabitha (Dorcas) to life (9:36–42). In like manner, Paul cured a man crippled from birth (14:8–18). People were healed by touching a piece of cloth he had held (19:11–12). He too was able to bring someone back from the dead (20:9–12). As Peter was miraculously set free from prison (5:19; 12:3–19), so was Paul (16:25–34). Miracle after miracle confirmed the men and the message they proclaimed. Consider some more of the wonderful works of God:

The appearance of the resurrected Christ	Acts 1:3
The sound of wind, fire, & the gift of languages	
The earth quaked in answer to prayer	Acts 4:31
Judgment fell upon Ananias and Sapphira	Acts 5:5–10
The resurrected Christ appeared to Saul	Acts 9:3–9
At the word from Ananias, sight was restored	
Peter healed Aeneas in Lydda	Acts 9:32–35
An angel appeared to Cornelius	Acts 10:3, 46
A sorcerer was blinded	Acts 13:11–12
A cripple was healed at Lystra	Acts 14:8-18
A young man was raised from death in Troas	
A viper bit Paul in Melita but did no harm	Acts 28:3–6
Diseases were cured by Paul in Melita	Acts 28:8–9

There are many other details associated with Peter and Paul in the biblical narrative, for the story of these amazing days is told primarily through their lives. The first twelve chapters of Acts are concerned mainly with the *Apostle Peter*, the initial leader of the Jewish-Christian church in Jerusalem, and also the initial point of contact with the Gentile world through Cornelius. The second half of Acts is devoted to the ministry of the *Apostle Paul*, who was converted to Christ while seeking to persecute the saints in Damascus (9:1–19). His three missionary journeys and his journey to Rome in chains are covered in the narrative. Brief summaries of their lives and the concise outline provide an overview of the main events in the *Book of Acts*.

Section	Chapters
Empowered	1—2:41, *The baptism of the Holy Spirit*
Established	2:42—7, *The birth of the Church*
Extended	8, *Beyond Jerusalem*
Enlightened	9—12, *Inclusion of the Gentiles*
Enlarged	13—28, *Paul's missionary journeys*

The Powerful Personality of Peter

Of all the personalities in the New Testament, Peter appeals to many people because he is so very human. Peter is presented as a very emotional personality with a penchant for saying the right thing at the right time, and also for saying the wrong thing at the wrong time. He seemed willing to speak for others (cp. Mark 8:29) and to ask the questions that everyone wanted to ask (Mark 10:28; 11:21; Matt. 15:15; 18:21; Luke 12:41). Four names are used to refer to Peter. He is called by his Hebrew name *Simeon* in Acts 15:14. The Greek equivalent *Simon* is used almost fifty times in the Gospels and Acts. Paul enjoyed calling him *Cephas* (cp. 1 Cor. 1:12; 2:22; 9:5), though *Peter* is employed most often.

Many things are known about Peter. He is the son of Jonah (John) according to Matthew 16:17 (cp. John 1:42). He and his brother Andrew were partners in a fishing business in Galilee (Mark 1:16; Luke 5:2–3; John 21:3) with James and John, the sons of Zebedee (Luke 5:10). Peter was married (Mark 1:29–31; 1 Cor. 9:5), and had a residence in Capernaum (Mark 1:21, 29). Prior to receiving the call to follow Jesus, Peter had been a disciple of John the Baptist (John 1:35–42).

As a disciple of Christ, the name of Peter is listed first in the apostolic roster (Mark 3:16; Luke 6:14; Matt. 10:2). Such preference is appropriate because Peter was a leader among men. He was sometimes singled out for special recognition (Mark 8:29–33), and enjoyed private moments with the Lord. Peter was present when Jesus raised a little girl to health (Mark 5:35–41), at the Transfiguration (Mark 9:2–8), and when Jesus was praying in the Garden of Gethsemane (Mark 14:43–50).

The worst moment in Peter's life came when he denied the Lord of glory (Mark 14:66–72). However, he was restored to fellowship and given a place of leadership in the Church of Jesus Christ (Matt. 16:17–19; John 21:15–19; Mark 16:7) in Jerusalem. His wise counsel and leadership allowed him to serve as a unifying force between those who ministered to the Jews and those who ministered to the Gentiles (Acts 10–11).

Tradition says that Peter died a witness for the Lord in Rome sometime after A.D. 60. His spiritual legacy includes the telling of his story to John Mark, who wrote his gospel and assisted with the two epistles, 1 and 2 Peter.

A Summary of Saul's Salvation

Like many Jewish babies, he had been named Saul, perhaps in memory of Israel's first king. Today, he is better known as Paul (meaning *little one*), indicating the change of his name (cp. Acts 13:9). Born of Jewish parents from the tribe of Benjamin who were also Roman citizens, Paul was reared in the city of Tarsus, Cilicia. According to both custom and Jewish law, he was circumcised on the eighth day. As a youth, it would be his privilege to sit at the feet of the great Rabbi Gamaliel and learn the Law of Moses. A capable student filled with religious zeal, Paul became "a Hebrew of the Hebrews" (Phil. 3:5). His fervor for the things he loved so dearly would find a terrible outlet: Paul persecuted those Christians of "The Way" until he was converted to Christ himself, *c.* A.D. 34. One of the scenes which haunted Paul throughout his life was the part he played in the death of Stephen. While others threw the stones which broke his body, Saul stood by and held their garments in consent.

Soon after his salvation, Paul began to preach Christ with the same intensity that he had once reserved for the Law. For Paul, the Law had lost its vitality and validity. He was given to understand that no one can be saved by keeping the Law. Only faith in Christ would save. There was more. Paul came to understand that if belief in Christ was the true object of saving faith, then even the Gentiles could believe. Paul would go and preach to the Gentiles. His initial work took him to such places as Damascus, and then to the kingdom of the Nabatean Arabs to the east and south. While there is no record of the details of his activity in Arabia (Gal. 1:17), some opposition was involved, for the "governor" of King Aretas in Damascus sought to have him arrested (2 Cor. 11:32–33).

After returning from Damascus, Paul went to Jerusalem to meet Peter and James, the Lord's brother (Gal. 1:18–19). Because of intense hostility against Paul by the Jews (his former associates), he had to flee the city. He was taken to Caesarea on the Mediterranean coast to board a boat for Tarsus. For ten years Paul would evangelize the Gentiles.

At the end of this period, Barnabas came to Tarsus from Antioch to invite Paul to join him in caring for a thriving church there. A year later, Paul and Barnabas visited Jerusalem to confer with Peter, James, and John (Gal. 2:10). The result of this meeting was an agreement that those in Jerusalem would focus attention on evangelizing to the Jews, while Barnabas and Paul would take the gospel to the Gentiles. Because of the famine in the city, it was requested that Barnabas and Paul try to find ways to send financial relief whenever possible.

Three Missionary Journeys

Encouraged by the church at Antioch to take the gospel to the Gentile world, Barnabas and Paul set out in A.D. 47 on the first of three missionary journeys. In A.D. 48/49, Barnabas and Paul returned to Jerusalem to ask counsel regarding the proper relationship between the Jews and

Gentiles. It was decided that while circumcision should not be imposed upon the Gentile converts, they should conform to certain aspects of the Jewish law in order to keep peace (Acts 15:1–29).

Once that question was settled, Paul and Barnabas parted company over the controversial behavior of John Mark. Paul chose Silas to travel with him. Together they visited the developing churches of Galatia. At Lystra, they were joined by Timothy, whom Paul had led to Christ two years earlier.

Planning to journey west to Ephesus, the Holy Spirit led them instead to turn north and northwest and go to the seaport of Troas. In a vision, Paul was led of the Lord to go to Macedonia. With the addition of Luke to their small group (Acts 16:10), the four men moved on to Macedonia to the Roman colony of Philippi; there the Lord established a church despite strong opposition. From Philippi the journey was made to Thessalonica, the major city of the province, where a church was established. However, when a riot broke out, the four missionaries were forced to leave the city in haste.

Paul moved next to Berea where he was well received, but opponents from Thessalonica had followed him there. So much unrest was created that the journey had to continue. Paul was forced to flee from city to city. Alone now, Paul moved south into the province of Achaia where he briefly stayed in Athens, and then went to Corinth in fear for his life (1 Cor. 2:3). Despite his initial apprehensions, Paul stayed for 18 months and saw many souls come to the Savior. While he was at Corinth, a new Roman proconsul named Gallio arrived on July 1, A.D. 51, to take up residence in the wicked metropolitan city. When Paul was brought before Gallio on charges of preaching an illegal religion, the proconsul dismissed the charges.

From Corinth, Paul returned to Jerusalem and Antioch before going to Ephesus, where he would remain for three years. The Lord gave Paul and those who ministered with him many souls for their labors in the whole province of Asia (western Asia Minor). As the great apostle considered his next move, he wanted to go to Spain (Rom. 15:20). Such a journey would give him the opportunity to go through Rome. But before that could happen, Paul felt he needed to take a love offering to the saints back in Jerusalem. Though apprehensive of being arrested (Rom. 15:25–32), he made the journey anyway, only to be attacked by a mob near the Temple. Though Roman soldiers came to his rescue, Paul was kept in custody for the next two years. After appealing to Caesar, he was sent to Rome in chains in the fall of A.D. 59. Two more years would pass before his case came before the Imperial Court. Still, he was able to proclaim the gospel to all he met (Phil. 1:2, 18). Because he was under house arrest, Paul was able to receive visitors, including Epaphroditus from Philippi and Epaphras from Colossae. From Colossae, too, came Onesimus, the slave of his friend Philemon (Phil. 1:6).

About the remainder of Paul's life there is little information. It is probable that he was released from prison only to be incarcerated a second time, and to suffer martyrdom under the Roman emperor Nero. The probable site of his execution can still be visited today at Tre Fontane on the Ostain Road. A burial place is marked near the Basilica of St. Paul. Beneath a high altar is a stone inscription carved at least in the fourth century: "TO PAUL, APOSTLE AND MARTYR."

Major Events during the Days of Paul

4 B.C.	Herod the Great, King of Judea from 37 to 4 B.C.	
4	Archelaus Ethnarch of Judea/Idumaea/Samaria 4 B.C. to 6 A.D.	
4	Philip Tetrarch of Batanaea, Trachionitis, Auranitis and "Ituraea" 4 B.C. to 6 A.D.	
4	Lysanias Tetrarch of Abilene in Syria 4 BC to A.D. 37	
A.D. 6	Judea made a Roman province under a procurator	
c. 10	Paul is born in the city of Tarsus	Acts 22:3
14	Tiberius Caesar becomes Roman Emperor, rules to A.D. 37	
18	Caiaphas becomes the Jewish High Priest and remains in office until A.D. 36.	

	(Jesus appeared before him)	Matt. 26:57–68
c. 20–30	Paul is educated in Judaism	Acts 22:3
26	Pontus Pilate becomes Procurator of Judea and remains in office until 36 A.D.	
	(Jesus appeared before him)	Matt. 27:2–26
27	Appearance of John the Baptist, baptism of Jesus and the beginning of the public ministry of Christ	
30	Crucifixion of Jesus	
30	Pentecost and pouring out of the Spirit during the days when Tiberius was Emperor of Rome and Pontius Pilate was still the Procurator of Judea	
31	Spread of the gospel at Jerusalem	
35–40	The conversion of Cornelius	Acts 10
35–36	Paul persecuted Christians	
36	Martyrdom of Stephen witnessed by Paul	Acts 7:58
	Death of Tiberius, accession of Emperor Caius Caligula (he rules until A.D. 41). Pilate deposed.	
	Herod Agrippa I given the tetrarchy of Philip and Abilene	
37	Conversion of Saul	Acts 9
38	Paul goes into Arabia	Gal. 1:17
	Herod Agrippa I is relieved of his duties	
39	Paul visits Jerusalem	Acts 9:26–29
	Paul returns to Tarsus	Acts 9:30
	Herod Antipas is banished to Gaul	
	Dominions of Herod Antipas given to Herod Agrippa I.	
	Emperor Caligula orders his statue to be set up at Jerusalem leading to a riot.	
40	The revolt of Theudas takes place	Acts 5:36
41	Peter goes on a missionary journey	
	Cornelius is converted	Acts 10—11
42	Herod Agrippa I is made King of Judea and Samaria.	

	Claudius succeeds Caligula as Roman Emperor, rules until A.D. 54	
	The gospel spreads as far as Antioch	
43	Paul is brought to Antioch	Acts 11:25–26
44	Persecution of Christians by Herod Agrippa	
	The killing of James with the sword	
	Herod Agrippa imprisons Peter	
	Death of Herod Agrippa (Cuspius Fadus, Procurator)	
	Beginning of conquest of Britain by the Romans	
45	Famine in Judea as prophesied by Agabus Acts 11:28–31	

The First Missionary Journey

A.D. 45	First missionary journey	
	Cyprus	Acts 13:4–12
	Perga	Acts 13:13
46	Pisidian Antioch	Acts 13:14–50
	Iconium	Acts 13:51–14:5
	Lystra	Acts 14:6–19
	Derbe	Acts 14:20
47	Paul & Barnabas return to Lystra, Iconium, Pisidian Antioch	
		Acts 14:21–24
	Tiberius Alexander is Procurator	
	Perga, Attalia	Acts 14:25
46–48	Claudius expels the Jews from Rome	
	Paul is resisted at Antioch	Acts 14:26–28
48	Ventidius Cumanus is made Procurator of Judea	
50	The Council at Jerusalem	Acts 15

The Second Missionary Journey

A.D. 50	Paul's 2nd missionary journey with Silas Acts 16–18
50	Paul goes to Antioch by land through Syria and Cilicia Acts 15:41

	Derbe and Lystra	Acts 16:1–5
	Phrygia and Galatia	Acts 16:6
	Troas, Samothrace, Neapolis, Philippi	Acts 16:8–40
51	Gallio becomes Proconsul of Achaia	Acts 18:12
	Paul arrives at Thessalonica	Acts 17:1–9
	Athens	Acts 17:15–34
52	Paul arrives at Corinth	Acts 18:1–17
	1 and 2 Thessalonians written	
	Felix becomes Procurator of Judea, until A.D. 59	
53	Paul leaves Corinth and sails to Ephesus, Caesarea and Jerusalem to Feast of Tabernacles	Acts 18:18–22
53/54	Return of Paul to Antioch	Acts 18:22

The Third Missionary Journey

A.D. 54	Death of Claudius; accession of Nero and rule to A.D. 68	
	Paul starts third missionary journey	Acts 19, 20
	To Galatia and Phrygia	Acts 18:23
54–57	Residence and preaching of Paul at Ephesus	Acts 19
57	Writing of 1 and 2 Corinthians, Romans, Galatians	
	Paul leaves Ephesus in June	1 Cor. 16:8
	for Troas	Acts 20:6–12
	and then Miletus	Acts 20:13–38
58	Paul leaves Corinth for Jerusalem	Acts 21:1–17
	Stops at Philippi, leaves in April	Acts 20:6
	Reaches Jerusalem in June, arrested in the Temple	Acts 20:16
58–60	Spends the summer A.D. 58 to fall A.D. 60 in Caesarea	Acts 23:23—26:32
	Waiting for a trial before Felix	
58	Nero murders Agrippa; recall of Felix; Porcius Festus is Procurator	
57–59	Nero murders his wife and mother	

59	Paul interviewed by Felix
	Porcius Festus becomes Procurator of Judea
60	Paul appears before Festus and Agrippa
	Paul makes his appeal to Caesar
	Paul sets sail for Rome, is shipwrecked at Malta Acts 27—28
	Travels on to Caesarea, Sidon, Cyprus, Myra, Cnidus, Salmone, Fair Havens, Phenice, Clauda, Syrtis, Adria, Malta, Melita, Syracuse, Regium, Puteoli, Appii Forum, The Three Taverns, Rome.
61–63	Paul reaches Rome, lives in his own house for two years
62	Writing of: Philippians, Colossians, Philemon, Ephesians
64-67?	The First Trial (and acquittal of Paul?)
	Writing of Epistles: 1 Timothy, Titus, Hebrews(?)
	To Spain perhaps, or Crete? Titus 1:5
	To Asia? 2 Tim. 4:13
	To Macedonia? 2 Tim. 4:20
	Earthquake at Pompeii; Albinus is Procurator
	Paul passes the winter at Nicopolis Titus 3:12, 15
64	Rome burns; Christians flee to Pella Rev. 12:14
65	Paul journeys through Macedonia to Troas
	Paul is arrested for the second time and sent to Rome
c. 66	Paul is tried before the Emperor of Rome
67	Writing of Second Epistle to Timothy
68	Martyrdom of Paul
	Jewish war begins; massacre at Jerusalem; repulse of Cestius Gallus
	Death of Nero, extinction of the house of the Caesars
70	Jerusalem falls to Tiberius' Roman Legions under Titus

The Acts of the Apostles: An Outline

I. 1:1—8:3 The Church in Jerusalem
    A. Waiting for the Wind   1:1–22
    B. The Matter of Matthias   1:23–26
    C. The Power of Pentecost   2:2–47
    D. "Signs and Wonders"   3:1—4:37
    E. Judgment in the House of God   5:1–42
    F. The Selection of Seven Servants   6:1–15
    G. Standing Up for Stephen   7:1—8:3

II. 8:4—11:18 The Church to Judea and Samaria
    A. The Preaching of Philip   8:4–40
    B. The Salvation of Saul   9:1–43
    C. The Conversion of Cornelius   10:1—11:18

III. 11:19—28:31 The Church to the World
    A. The Gospel Arrives in Antioch   11:19–28
    B. Gifts of God's Grace   11:29–30
    C. The Hatred of Herod Agrippa I   12:1–25
    D. Divine Guidance for Barnabas and Saul   13:1–3
    E. The Gospel Is Proclaimed to the Gentiles   13:4–12

Paul's First Missionary Journey A.D. 45–48
    F. The Terrible Mistake of John Mark   13:13
    G. Antioch, Iconium, Lystra, and Derbe   13:14–14:28

The Council Meeting at Jerusalem A.D. 50
    H. A Question of Conscience   15:1–35

Paul's Second Missionary Journey A.D. 50–53
    I. "Son of Consolation"   15:36–39

J.	Silas: Co-laborer with Paul	15:40–41
K.	Young Timothy	16:1–3
L.	The Gospel Reaches Europe	16:4–9
M.	Paul at Philippi	16:10-40
N.	"Turning the World Upside Down"	17:1–14
O.	Athens: The Cradle of Democracy	17:15–34
P.	A Return to Spiritual Roots	18:1–28

Paul's Third Missionary Journey A.D. 54–58

Q.	Three Years at Ephesus	19:1–12
R.	The Debate over Diana	19:13–41
S.	A Journey of Love	20:1—21:16
T.	Danger in the City of Peace	21:17—26:32
U.	The Last Voyage to Rome	27:1—28:15
V.	Two Years at Rome A.D. 61–63	28:16–31

9

Faith Alone

THE EPISTLE OF PAUL TO THE ROMANS

Written A.D. 58
Key word: "Faith"

"For I am not ashamed of the gospel of Christ: for it is the power of God unto salvation to every one that believeth; to the Jew first, and also to the Greek. For therein is the righteousness of God revealed from faith to faith: as it is written, The just shall live by faith."

—Romans 1:16–17

The Apostolic Author

The fourteen letters of the New Testament which Paul wrote met a variety of needs. Some letters, such as *1* and *2 Corinthians, Galatians, Ephesians, Philippians,* and *1* and *2 Thessalonians,* served to encourage, warn, and instruct the believers in their new faith in the Lord Jesus Christ. Other letters, such as *Romans* and *Colossians,* were written to set forth great doctrinal truths. Still others were written to instruct individuals on practical matters, as *Timothy, Titus,* and *Philemon* in this manner. Together, the Pauline Epistles form a solid foundation for faith and practice in the churches today. They are a treasury of guidance for us from God.

In many Pauline epistles a definite pattern may be observed. There is the introduction whereby Paul identifies himself and those to whom he is writing. This is followed by a general greeting and the giving of thanks. Doctrinal issues are then discussed, and then there is personal application. Herbert Lockyer comments that, "Wise preachers who desire to exercise an effective ministry must emulate the apostolic method of first preaching doctrine, then making the application." The same is true for every believer in spiritual growth.

Having a pastoral heart, Paul was always burdened for his brethren (1 Thess. 2:1–10). He was committed to praying for their spiritual growth (Eph. 1 & 3; Phil. 1:8–11). A concluding section in Paul's letters extends specific greetings, and then a benediction—that the grace of God might rest upon His people (cp. Rom. 16:24; 1 Cor. 16:23; Phil. 4:23; 1 Thess. 5:28; 2 Thess. 3:18).

In the early part of several letters, Paul liked to evoke the grace and peace of God (cp. Rom. 1:7; Gal. 1:3). *Grace* and *peace* are two great words of the New Testament. The word *grace* speaks of unmerited favor freely bestowed, while *peace* speaks of the cessation of hostility. Man receives God's grace through the Lord Jesus Christ, resulting in eternal life and freedom from the power and pollution of sin, which brings him peace.

A Chronology of Paul's Letters	Written
During Second Missionary Journey - 1 Thessalonians, 2 Thessalonians;	A.D. 50–53
During Third Missionary Journey, - Galatians, 1 Corinthians, 2 Corinthians, Romans;	A.D. 54–58
During (First) Roman Imprisonment, - Colossians, Ephesians, Philemon, Philippians, (Hebrews);	A.D. 61–63

> During (Prior to Second) Roman Imprisonment,   A.D. 64–67
> - 1 Timothy, Titus, 2 Timothy.

Why Written: Motives of a Missionary

One purpose for Paul's writing to the believers in the royal city was preparatory. It was the Apostle's intention to pass through Macedonia and Achaia, and then visit Jerusalem before going to Rome (Acts 19:21). In preparation for this ultimate objective, Paul wrote his letter. It was carried from Corinth in the hands of a lady named Phoebe, a woman from Cenchrea (near Corinth, Acts 18:18), who was traveling to Rome (Rom. 16:1).

Paul had friends in Rome, reflected in the numerous personal names of Romans 16. He had tried often to visit the brethren (15:23; 1:13), but was unsuccessful in his efforts. The church was composed mainly of Gentiles (1:13) who were not well informed of the things of Christ (Acts 28:21). There were some Jews in the assembly, but not many. Most Jews had been banished from the city by Claudius, the fourth Roman emperor (ruler, A.D. 41 to 54).

The origin of the church in Rome is uncertain. It is possible that the beginnings of the church can be traced to the day of Pentecost. There were present in Jerusalem "sojourners from Rome" (Acts 2:10). It may be that some of the people present that day heard the gospel and came to faith in Jesus Christ. They returned to Rome and established a local assembly. Aquila and Priscilla were among this group (Acts 16:3). There is no evidence in the New Testament that Peter had anything to do with founding the church in Rome.

As Paul contemplated going to the imperial city, there were several factors which motivated him. First, the opportunity to preach Christ to the multitudes existed in Rome. As people came to faith, Paul knew that they would carry the gospel message back to their nations and communities, so that the good news of Christ would spread to the ends of the earth (cp. Acts 13:47; Rom. 10:18; Col. 1:6). Rome would be added to Antioch, Ephesus, and Philippi as a great focal point of missionary outreach. Second, Paul wanted to end the activities of the Judaizers in Rome. Paul wanted Jesus, and not the Jewish religion, to have the preimminence. To this end, he would visit the city and preach Christ. However, before his visit, Paul would write a pastoral and doctrinal epistle stating in a full and systematic way the essence of Christian theology—summarized in one great theme: the righteousness of God in the justification of men by faith alone (Rom. 1:16-17).

Overview of Romans

From Ruin to Redemption (1—5)

The righteousness of God stands in contrast to the righteousness of man. The Jews believed that righteousness consisted in keeping the Law of Moses. The Gentiles believed that righteousness consisted of observing an ethical code of moral conduct. Paul reveals that the righteousness of God is found in the Person and work of the Lord Jesus Christ. Paul will employ precise terms to elaborate on this great theme of Divine righteousness. He will teach about justification, imputation, adoption, and sanctification.

The great theme of chapters 1 and 2 is that the righteousness of God is needed because men are completely unrighteous and without excuse since God has revealed Himself to them. Jews and Gentiles alike (i.e., all men) stand guilty before God so that "there is none righteous, no not one" (Rom. 3:10). Since the whole world is helpless and condemned, a legal and personal righteousness can only be found in Christ, "whom God set forth to be a propitiation [wrath satisfaction], through faith in his blood, to show his righteousness because of the passing over of the sins done aforetime" (Rom. 3:25). Since no person can earn or deserve salvation, righteousness is granted by God out of His grace and mercy.

Sinners receive Christ's righteousness by faith in the substitutionary death of Christ at Calvary. He who was without sin died the death due the sinner, so that the believing sinner might live the blessed life due Christ.

From the Self-life to the Christ-life (6—8)

Here Paul explains that the new life of the believer is a totally new life—the life of Christ in him via the Spirit. It is a life completely identified (Greek, *baptizo*) with Christ: His thoughts, His desires, His will, His ways—instead of one's own. The believer is able to walk in victory because he is now free through Christ to say "no" to the power of sin. These chapters are especially worth studying: ch. 6 is the believer's identification with Christ in His death, burial, and resurrection; ch. 7 is the futility of trying to keep the law in our own strength; and ch. 8 is the beauty of the victorious Christian life in the Spirit.

Also, some personal and practical problems are contemplated on the basis of an imputed (given by God apart from men's works) righteousness by faith. For example: if sin causes grace to be manifested, "shall we continue in sin, that grace may abound?" ("No", Rom. 6:1). "Shall we sin, because we are not under Law, but under grace?" ("No", 6:15). Paul, "is the Law sin?" ("No", 7:7). And Paul, if the Law is sin, "who shall deliver me out of this body of death?" ("Christ alone", 7:24). The answers to these questions all point to Christ and personal, practical holiness—in some of the most beautiful language ever written. Someone has said, "*Romans* is the great cathedral of truth in the Bible; chapter 8 is its central spire."

From Gentile to Jew (9—11)

From the personal life of the believer, Paul turns to address in Romans 9—11 God's covenant relationship with Israel, which had initially been established by the Law. The central question is this: "What place does

Israel have in the Divine economy?" Paul will respond by reviewing the sovereignty of God, the sinfulness of man, and the consequences of personal and national transgressions. He will make important distinctions between the racial, religious, and regenerate Jew.

From Duty to Devotion (12—16)

Then, having discussed the future and fate of national and spiritual Israel, the Apostle will make an appeal to ethical behavior (Rom. 14:8–9). Obedience to God's principles must govern the daily walk of the true believer—out of a motive of love for Him. Of particular importance are ch. 13 (submission to authority) and ch. 14 (guidance in "doubtful things"—gray areas where Scripture does not give an absolute command).

The conclusion of the *Epistle to the Romans* (15:14–33) sets forth Paul's terrestrial tactics. He will take the gospel to that part of the world where Christ is not known (15:20). He will offer hope to the heathen and knowledge to those who sit in spiritual darkness. He will work and he will write wonderful words of doctrinal and practical truth, so that all men might have, as William Tyndale said, "a light and way into the whole Scriptures."

10

The Cross for the Church

THE FIRST EPISTLE OF PAUL TO THE CORINTHIANS

Written A.D. 57
Key word: "Cross"

"For the preaching of the Cross is to them that perish foolishness; but unto us which are saved it is the power of God."

—1 Corinthians 1:18

A City Called Corinth

Originally a Phoenician settlement, Corinth enjoyed an ancient history. The Greeks came to dominate the city and the region. In 146 B.C., Corinth was destroyed by the legions of Rome. One hundred years later, in 46 B.C., the Romans rebuilt the city in pure white marble under the imperial order of Julius Caesar.

When the Apostle Paul first reached the splendid reconstructed city in the autumn of A.D. 51 on his Second Missionary Journey (A.D. 50–53), it was a thriving metropolis (Acts 18). Located 50 miles west of Athens on the southern extremity of the Isthmus of Corinth (the narrow strip of land which connects northern and southern Greece), Corinth provided natural harbors through which flowed the commerce of the world. Corinth became one of the largest (pop. 200,000 plus a half million slaves), wealthiest, and most important cities of the Empire. Only Rome, Alexandria, and Antioch surpassed it in significance.

Romans, Jews, and other nationalities dwelt within the larger Greek population to enjoy financial prosperity, sensual pleasure, and spiritual ignorance. They allowed both pagan polytheism and idolatry. They had an idol for every god and a god for every facet of life. On a mountain high above the city, a magnificent temple of white marble had been built to Aphrodite, the Greek goddess of love and beauty, known to the Romans as Venus.

The women who served in the temple as priestesses were really professional prostitutes. One thousand were available on ordinary occasions, and fifteen hundred were available for special festivals. People said of Corinth that it was, "A renowned and voluptuous city, where the vices of East and West met."

Paul in the Province

Paul was destined to turn this unholy city "upside down" (Acts 17:6) and then "right side up," with the preaching of the gospel of redeeming grace. For eighteen months the Apostle labored to establish a church, all the while ministering with great fear and trembling (1 Cor. 2:3). Paul had known opposition in Athens and he was apprehensive that he would find the same in Corinth. To encourage his heart, the Lord promised Paul that many souls would be saved (Acts 18:9–10; 1 Thess. 2:17–18). He was to stay and preach openly and boldly.

While in Corinth, Paul initially lodged in the home of Aquila and Priscilla. He worked as a tent-maker because he did not want his motives to be questioned. He did not want to be known as a greedy man or a person who was trying to *make money* from ministry to God's people (a principle much needed in this day). So he worked with his own hands to support himself.

In time, Silas and Timothy joined Paul at Corinth. Timothy had some good news concerning the believers at Thessalonica (1 Thess. 3:6): the church there was doing well. Meanwhile, Paul preached every Sabbath in the synagogue in Corinth—despite open hostility from the Jews. After a devout Gentile named Titus Justus offered him the use of his home which was next to the synagogue, Paul was able to see souls come to the Savior, including Crispus, the ruler of the synagogue and his household. Of those who came to faith, Paul only baptized Crispus and Gaius (a host during a latter visit, Rom. 16:23), and the household of Stephanas (1 Cor. 16:15). Though baptism is important, Paul felt that preaching was more important (1:14–17).

In the spring of A.D. 53, Paul left the city of Corinth in order to go to Jerusalem and Antioch (in Syria). He wanted to confer with the leaders of the church at Jerusalem and then give a report to the brethren in Antioch on the work of his ministry. The following year, A.D. 54, Paul sailed from Antioch to begin his Third Missionary Journey. As he ventured westward, he visited again the churches in Galatia, and finally came to the capital city of Ephesus in Asia Minor. Ephesus would be the center of his ministry for the next three years. Because the lines of communication were well established due to quality Roman roads, he could easily interact with the church of Corinth, which was 200 miles west across the Aegean Sea. The Apostle wanted to know how the believers were doing. He soon found out and was made sad.

Why Written: To Admonish and to Answer

We read of "persons of the household of Chloe" (1 Cor. 1:11) coming from Corinth to Paul with reports of wicked behavior in the assembly. The saints in the notorious "Sin City" had not remained distinct from the culture around them. Paul looked for the Church in the world—and found the world in the Church! With anguish of heart, he wrote a quick letter to the church, which has been lost (cp. 1 Cor. 5:9). We do know that the letter strongly rebuked the righteous ones for the sin they had allowed to saturate their lives and pollute others (2 Cor. 2:3–4, 9).

Having sent the "lost" letter quickly, Paul wanted to know how his words had been received. Would the believers respond and repent, or would they react in anger and hostility? No word had been yet forthcoming from Timothy, whom Paul had sent to Corinth through Macedonia.

Finally, other believers arrived from Corinth. They were led by Stephanas, Fortunatus, and Achaicus (1 Cor. 16:17). From them and from a letter they brought (note 7:1), Paul was able to discern more clearly the whole situation in the church. It was not altogether good. The people still had a number of practical and spiritual questions that needed addressing. His letter back to them, then, centers around two areas: (1) he *admonishes* them to correct some real problems that he saw (chs. 1—6) and (2) he *answers* their questions about many church practices (chs. 7—16).

Overview of 1 Corinthians

Divisions and Disorders (1—6)

With apostolic authority and a pastor's heart, Paul first instructs the church about several problems he had seen.

Chapters 1—4 (Divisions)

The Corinthians were favoring one man over another! Paul proceeded to teach about: sectarianism (1:10–16), arrogant "human wisdom" (which is leaning upon one's own understanding, rather than relying upon God, 1:17–31), the wisdom of God (2:1–31), and carnality (3:1–22). Regarding human wisdom, Paul is not anti-intellectual; but he insists that we should train our minds, and submit them to Christ's direction.

The "Carnal Christian" Theory. The passage on *carnality* is very important to understand. The carnal are "babes in Christ" who by intellect and self-will try to please God in doing His work. They are "fleshly," relying on their senses and their own strength, rather than the Spirit and God's strength. In addition to the truly spiritual and these carnal "babes," some mistakenly suppose there is a third group: those who have prayed to receive Christ, but live as still in the flesh—pursuing their own desires and will. Their lifestyles are similar to those in the world, where marks of salvation are the exception rather than the rule. Are they truly saved, or are they terribly deceived? The Scriptures point to "carnal" being limited to only temporary backsliding, where God brings grief over sin (as David in the Psalms) or chastening (as in Hebrews 12), in order to turn the true Christian back to a holy walk as a normal lifestyle (1 Cor. 6:9–11; 1 John 2:3–4,15; 2 Cor. 5:17). Thus, those living a "carnal" <u>lifestyle</u> are *not* saved, and Paul exhorts us to "examine yourselves" (2 Cor. 13:5).

In chapter 4, Paul vindicated his own ministry—some had refused to accept his authority. They displayed an emotional revolt of the soul against reason and spiritual maturity (2 Cor. 11:12–23).

Chapters 5—6 (Disorders)

Here Paul goes on to address other problems: the incredible case of incest (5:1–13), going to court (6:1–8), and sexual indulgence (6:9–20).

At the heart of every one of the Corinthian problems was this: they had slid into a self-centered life. The answer to every problem, then, was found in one focus—Paul brings them back to the cross: a life of self-renunciation in order to exalt Christ.

Difficulties (7—14)

After chastising them for errors, Paul turns to answer some of their own questions, put to him via the visitors from Corinth.

Chapter 7 (Marriage)

Chapter 7 is about desires regarding marriage (7:10–40). Though Paul was not married at this time (7:8), some Bible scholars believe that he had been married earlier. Two reasons are offered. First, Paul voted in the Sanhedrin (Acts 26:10), where it is understood that marriage was a necessary prerequisite. Second, the style of writing indicates someone who has known the sensitivities of married life.

Chapters 8—10 (Doubtful Things)

The apostolic counsel continues concerning support of the work of the ministry and ministers (9:1-14), the danger of falling away (9:15-27), and eating meats sacrificed to idols (8:1-9, cp. 10:14-33). Here is some of the clearest guidance regarding the things about which Scripture does not specifically command as either right or wrong, i.e., *gray areas.* Instead of "freedom to do as we please" as long as it does not violate a specific command, we have: "all things are lawful, but all are not expedient" (10:23a), "all things do not edify" (10:23b), do not cause a brother to stumble (10:28), and "do all to the glory of God" (10:31). These are wonderful principles to guide us toward holy conduct in every affair of life.

Chapter 11 (Ministry and Worship [communion])

Paul includes other topics: guidance about the role of women in the church, and abuses at the Lord's Table (11:20-34). Some interpret his comments regarding women as cultural, and therefore not literally applicable to the Church today. Others see here an important principle: that a woman must always be in submission to the headship of male leaders (especially in church worship)—not suggesting comparative weakness, but a simple distinction and clarification of roles in order to maintain orderly functioning and growth. In addition, communion with the saints at the Lord's Table must always be done in an atmosphere of *agape* love.

Chapters 12—14 (Spiritual Gifts)

Paul here deals with the proper place and use of spiritual gifts (12:1–31), speaking in tongues (14:1–33), and the use of ecstatic utterances (14:34-40). These chapters contain clear guidance for how to avoid the excesses which can occur in the practice of charismatic sign gifts (tongues and prophecy). They are neither the normal nor necessary sign of the filling of the Holy Spirit.

Included in the midst of his presentation is the great chapter on Christian love (13:1–13). *Agape* love is the love of God toward us: unmerited (totally undeserved by us) and unconditional (without requiring our "performance" to earn God's favor). The solution to all issues in the body of Christ is first of all the practice of Christ's *agape* love toward one another.

Direction (15—16)

Chapter 15 is the beautiful Resurrection chapter, one of the high points of the New Testament (15:1–58). The bodily resurrection of Christ from death in the grave is fundamental to the gospel (15:1–11) and to our entire faith (15:12–19). If there is no resurrection, then it is foolishness to share in Christ's suffering and self-denial. Christ's resurrection is proof of His victory over death, and of God's acceptance of His perfect sacrifice.

Paul then discusses the gathering of a love offering to be given to the suffering saints in Jerusalem (16:1–3; cp. 2 Cor. 8:10). There was a wonderful response to this appeal for financial help (2 Cor. 9:2–5). The letter ends with salutation (16:19–24) and the Aramaic word *Maranatha*, meaning "Our Lord comes!" (cp. Rev. 22:20).

In the spring of A.D. 57, Paul sent his letter on to the church, hoping to visit them the following winter (16:5–8). When he did visit that winter (Acts 20:2–3), he wrote his *Epistle to the Romans* (Rom. 16:23). Many years later, c. A.D. 97, Clement of Rome wrote a letter to the church at Corinth. Its contents reveal that the Christian community was still plagued by divisions.

11

Ministry in the Church

The Second Epistle of Paul to the Corinthians

Written A.D. 58
Key word: "Ministry"

"Therefore, seeing we have this ministry; as we have received mercy, we faint not."
—2 Corinthians 4:1

Why Written: Hope and Healing

While on his Third Missionary Journey, Paul wrote a second epistle to the church at Corinth from Philippi in Macedonia. He had been waiting there to hear about the situation in Corinth. Finally, Titus arrived with some good news (cp. 1:3–4 with 7:6–7). The believers at Corinth had repented of their sins and were moving towards a better state of personal and corporate sanctification. After receiving this favorable report, Paul wrote his letter, which was probably delivered by Titus and two other brethren (2 Cor. 8:16–24).

For a long time, Paul had hoped to return to Corinth personally (note 1 Cor. 16:5–8). However, in the providence of the Lord, he had been required to remain almost three years at Ephesus (A.D. 54–57), trying to establish churches in the western section of Asia Minor. Now that the new churches were established, Paul felt he could fulfill the longing of his heart to return to the church at Corinth. He decided to remain in Ephesus only until Pentecost of June, A.D. 57. Then, he would make the journey to Macedonia, and from there to Greece, reaching Corinth by late autumn.

The epistle reveals the tremendous opposition Paul had to endure from the teachers of Judaism who had arrived in Corinth from Jerusalem. They had successfully sought to denounce Paul as not being a true minister of the gospel. This revolt had caused Paul to visit the church briefly, but without much effect (2 Cor. 12:14; 13:1–2). Now, things were different. Time had passed. Dark passions against Paul had subsided. The Holy Spirit had brought repentance to the hearts of many in the church, to the point that they removed from the fellowship those who had led the attack on Paul. The authority of Paul was restored and fully respected. Titus was probably instrumental in bringing about some of this change.

The Pain of Paul

Because relationships were partially restored, *The Second Epistle of Paul to the Corinthians* is the most personal of all Paul's letters. The Apostle opens his heart and shares his story with the saints. His life as an evangelist is detailed. Few knew of the great hardships Paul had endured and would yet endure for the sake of the Savior over a thirty-year time span. This is what is known about the sufferings of Paul:

(1) Men plotted to kill him in Damascus   Acts 9:24
(2) Others plotted to kill him in Jerusalem   Acts 9:29
(3) He was to be stoned in Iconium   Acts 14:5
(4) He was stoned and left for dead in Lystra   Acts 14:19
(5) In Philippi: beaten with rods and put in stocks Acts 16:23–24
(6) In Thessalonica a mob tried to destroy him   Acts 17:5

(7) He was driven out of Berea   Acts 17:13–14
(8) He was plotted against in Corinth   Acts 18:12
(9) In Ephesus he was almost killed   Acts 19:29
                                                          2 Cor. 1:8–9
(10) In Corinth again, shortly after writing
    2 Corinthians, his death was again plotted   Acts 20:3
(11) In Jerusalem, a mob would have killed Paul
    had not the Roman soldiers intervened   Acts 22
(12) He was imprisoned in Caesarea for two years.
(13) He was imprisoned in Rome for two more years.
(14) Unrecorded sufferings of beatings, imprisonment,
    shipwrecks, and personal privations   2 Cor. 11:23–27
(15) Finally, Paul was taken to Rome to be executed   2 Tim. 2:9

Paul was willing to endure all this and more for the sake of the gospel. He firmly believed that there was a greater glory to follow after the trials and tribulations of this life. He also believed that those who die before the coming of the Lord enter into a state of conscious blessedness to await the resurrection from the dead.

Overview of 2 Corinthians

Three main divisions may be recognized in 2 Corinthians. First, in chapters 1–5 Paul gives an account of his ministry, with thanks to God for strength in suffering (1:1–11). Second, in chapters 6–9 Paul comments on the ordeal through which the church has endured, and about the collection that had been taken for the poor in Jerusalem. This love offering had been going on in different churches for more than a year. Many principles on grace giving are expounded. Finally, in chapters 10–13 Paul defends his ministry against the personal opposition he has met with and vindicates his apostolic authority.

It can be noted that in chapters 1–9 the language is in the *past* tense. This might suggest that whatever trouble once existed between Paul and the people was now healed and everyone was at peace. But that is not the case. Chapters 10-13, written in the *present* or *future* tense, reveal that there were still lingering doubts. Paul still felt compelled to answer charges and defend his apostolic authority.

Paul's Account of His Ministry (1—5)

The epistle opens with Paul's usual salutation and expression of thanksgiving. No doubt, part of Paul's thanksgiving is that he escaped death in Ephesus (see Acts 19:23–41 with 2 Cor. 1:8–9). Then, with a true pastoral heart, Paul wants to comfort those who are now suffering. Moreover, he wants the church to know that he longs to visit with them soon (1:12—2:2). This information is followed by his thoughts on his earlier "lost" letter which were severe in nature (2:3–17).

Chapters 3–5 express a renewed defense of Paul's ministry—with all the joy and sorrows, all the thrills and threats that are associated with spiritual warfare in advancing the kingdom of God. In chapter 3, Paul draws a contrast between his ministry and those of his enemies. The gospel stands in stark contrast to the law.

The Gospel Contrasted with the Law

The Gospel	**The Law**
written on the heart	written on stone
of the Spirit	of the letter
unto life	unto death
unveiled	veiled
unto righteousness	unto condemnation
remains	passes away

To be clear, we are free from the Law as a merit system to earn God's favor (all fulfilled in Christ). But the Law remains as an essential revelation of the character of God and a necessary guide for holy living.

Paul's Appeal to His Converts (6—9)

In chapters 6–9, Paul exhorts the saints to keep themselves pure in body and in spirit, in order to live a holy life before God as good stewards of all that God has given.

Paul's Answer to His Critics (10—13)

In these chapters, Paul returns to a defense against false charges. The Apostle compares himself with his enemies in Corinth whom he calls "false prophets." Paul's main defense is that his life and work reveal what nature of man he is (chapter 12 in particular). Some of the things said about Paul were very personal in nature and very unkind (10:1, 10). His bodily appearance was attacked. While there is no description of Paul in the New Testament, there is a description, dating from the second century, that says Paul was short in stature, had curly hair, crooked legs, blue eyes, a long nose, and bushy eyebrows. Some scholars think that Paul had poor eyesight (*chronic ophthalmia*), which at times made him unattractive in appearance (note Gal. 6:11). It is no small fact, but a powerful spiritual truth, that God chose in Paul one who would be weak in the eyes of men, but spiritually mighty in the eyes of God (ref. 1 Samuel 16:7).

The section ends with tender expressions of love and peace (13:11–14). Paul wrote this epistle in the summer of A.D. 57. In the fall, he was finally able to return to Corinth, where he spent the winter. The following spring, he began his journey to Jerusalem.

12

Life in Liberty

THE EPISTLE OF PAUL TO THE GALATIANS

Written A.D. 54
Key word: "Liberty"

"Stand fast therefore in the liberty wherewith Christ hath made us free, and be not entangled again with the yoke of bondage."

—Galatians 5:1

Grace for the Gauls

In the third century B.C., a group of people called *Gauls* settled in the north central part of Asia Minor. They had originally migrated westward into Macedonia and Greece from north of the Black Sea. The Greeks called these new settlers *Galatai,* from which the name *Galatians* is derived. By 25 B.C. this section of Asia Minor and all its inhabitants had been taken over by the Romans under the rule of Augustus Caesar. Using the old Galatia as a base, Augustus added a section of Pontus on the northeast, part of Phrygia on the southwest, and most of Lyconia on the south to create a larger Roman province well known during the apostolic days. The southern and southwestern districts were heavily populated, politically important, and commercially prosperous.

Taking advantage of all these elements, the Apostle Paul and Barnabas founded churches in this strategic region during their First Missionary Journey (A.D. 45–48). Churches were established at Antioch of Pisidia, Iconium, Lystra, and Derbe (Acts 13:4—14:28). They were later visited during Paul's Second (Acts 16:1–5, c. A.D. 50) and Third Missionary Journeys (Acts 18:23, c. A.D. 54). The people in the local churches were converted Gauls.

Why Written: A Double-Minded Ministry

As a people, the Gauls were impetuous and precarious. One moment they were ready to worship Paul and Barnabas as gods, only to be ready to stone them to death in the next instance. When Paul was present with them, the gospel was received. However, as soon as Paul left and the Judaizers came, there was a willingness to embrace those new ideas. The result among the people was a great uncertainty of what was true. The Gauls were confused. Should they embrace a doctrine of salvation by grace through faith *alone*, or should they also be circumcised and observe the Jewish Law?

Initially, the Galatians had been received into the church apart from the rite of circumcision, and without any obligation to keep the Jewish ceremonial law. Baptism had been administered. But then something happened. Jewish Christians in the church at Antioch (who had come to faith but were also legalistic), challenged the practice of accepting Gentiles into the church without insisting that they observe the Jewish law (Acts 15:1). The situation became serious. The whole issue was debated and individuals took sides. To resolve the controversy, they sought counsel from the Jerusalem church in A.D. 50. A delegation was appointed by the church at Antioch to include Paul, Barnabas, and Titus (Gal. 2:1). These were to go before the Apostles and Elders at Jerusalem and ask for a decision.

At the Jerusalem Council, speeches were given by Peter, Paul, Barnabas, and James, the brother of Jesus. It was finally decided *not* to require Gentile converts to observe Jewish ceremonial law, nor submit to the rite of circumcision. A letter was sent to the church at Antioch to that effect by the hands of Barsabbas, Silas, Paul, and Barnabas (see Acts 14-15 and Gal. 1–2). The doctrine of God's *free grace* had survived the dangerous attempt of the Judaizers to add works as necessary for salvation.

Despite the decision of the Jerusalem Council, the local concerns did not diminish. Certain influential teachers of Judaism would not be silent. They continued to unsettle the minds of the Gentile Christians concerning their obligation to observe the Jewish customs and laws (in order to merit God's favor). When word reached Paul, he was righteously indignant. The glory of Jesus Christ was being taught to be insufficient for salvation. Faith plus observing the Jewish ceremonial law was said to be the way of salvation. Paul was so disturbed by this teaching that he personally wrote with his own hand the message he had in mind (normally Paul would have used a secretary—cp. Gal. 6:11).

Overview of Galatians

Another Gospel (1—2)

With barely a civil introduction, Paul begins to deal with this movement towards apostasy on the part of the Galatians (c. A.D. 58). He is astonished that the Galatians could be so soon removed from the doctrine of grace found in Jesus Christ. They have turned to "another [*heteros*, not of the same kind or category] gospel, which is not another" [*allos*, of the same kind]. There is much of which they must repent. Paul, as an authentic apostle, has a right to call the church to spiritual accountability (chapters 1–2). One of the key verses in the whole Bible for sanctification is here: "I am crucified with Christ: nevertheless I live; yet not I, but Christ liveth in me" (Gal. 2:20).

The True Gospel (3—4)

Once more Paul will instruct them again on the doctrine of salvation by faith in Jesus Christ alone (3:1—5:12). The role of the Law versus grace is clearly communicated using the examples of Abraham and the two women.

By contrasting the circumcised with the uncircumcised (chs. 1–2), faith with works (chs. 3–4), and walking in the Spirit with living in the flesh (chs. 5–6), Paul sets forth the true Christian life. He will prove that the true gospel of justification by faith does not allow for legalism, or salvation by an earned "works-righteousness."

Here Paul boldly sets forth the freedom that is to be found in Christ Jesus. The *Epistle to the Galatians* has been called the *Magna Carta* (lit. Great Charter) of Christian Liberty. It is Christ who sets the soul free from the bondage of rules and regulations. Those who would put any soul under religious human bondage do not understand spiritual truth or the way of salvation in any era. They do not understand that the Law was not given to save anyone. The purpose of the Law was to condemn sinful man and make him see his need for a Savior. The Law was only a caretaker until Christ came. The Law had no life to give. Only Christ can give life and that more abundantly. Christ gives life by grace through faith alone (cp. Eph. 2:8–9). No man has ever been justified by the works of the Law, but only through faith in the Lord Jesus Christ.

True Freedom (5—6)

Neither does the gospel allow for carnality (a selfish lifestyle) after one is saved. Sanctification is a Divine undertaking (5:16–18). As we are saved (by grace alone), so are we sanctified (by grace alone). Our obedience is in a motive of love for God, not to *earn* a reward.

The works of the flesh are listed (5:19–21), and in contrast, the fruit of the Spirit is set forth (5:22–26).

Works of the Flesh	Works of the Spirit
Adultery	Love
Fornication	Joy
Uncleanness	Peace
Lasciviousness	Long-suffering
Idolatry	Gentleness
Witchcraft	Goodness
Hatred	Faith
Variance	Meekness
Emulation (jealousy)	Temperance
Wrath	
Strife	
Sedition (division)	
Heresies	
Envying	
Murder	
Drunkenness	
Reveling	

The epistle concludes with an exhortation to apply the great doctrines of the faith to life, and then a benediction (5:13—6:18).

A War Between Two Women

An allegory is used to illustrate the truth of grace vs. law (4:19–31). For the fifth time, the impossibility of the believer being under the Law is considered (cp. 2:19–21; 3:1–3; 3:25–26; 4:4–6; 4:9–31). Hagar and her son, representing the Law, are set in opposition to Sarah and her son, representing Grace. Hagar reflects the Old Covenant of works, Sarah speaks of the New Covenant of Grace.

According to the terms of the Old Covenant (of Works of the Law) made on Mt. Sinai, the children of Hagar were slaves performing the rituals of the Law. The earthly Jerusalem ministered only to the children of the bond-woman who had been born after the flesh and thus into slavery. As slaves they were powerless to change their status and had nothing to offer but works.

The children of Sarah were the recipients of the New Covenant (of Grace). They found their freedom at Mt. Calvary and looked forward to a heavenly Jerusalem (cf. Heb. 12:18–24). As children of Grace, they were free according to promise. Born into freedom, the children of Grace enjoy the dignity of being sons and daughters, with privileges which they took by faith. The meaning of the allegory is scripturally explained (4:27–31).

Understanding the allegory will serve the Christian well, for in chapter 5 the exhortation is given to "Stand fast therefore in the liberty wherewith Christ hath made us free, and be not entangled again with the yoke of bondage." Christian freedom should lead to spiritual compassion. "Brethren, if a man be overtaken in a fault, ye which are spiritual, restore such an one in the spirit of meekness; consider thyself, lest thou also be tempted" (Gal. 6:1).

Weary with the debate with the legalist, Paul concludes Galatians with a personal word for dismissal of the issue. "From henceforth let no man trouble me: for I bear in my body the marks of the Lord Jesus" (6:17). The life of Paul proves that a person can hold to the doctrine of God's sovereignty and at the same time proclaim a free gospel of a free offer of free grace, without becoming lawless and licentious, careless and cold-hearted toward others.

13

Union with Christ

The Epistle of Paul to the Ephesians

Written c. A.D. 61
Keyword: "Union"

"Blessed be the God and Father of our Lord Jesus Christ, Who hath blessed us with all spiritual blessings in heavenly places in Christ."

—Ephesians 1:3

Why Written: Pastoral Concern

During his first imprisonment in Rome (A.D. 61–63) Paul wrote several letters that have been preserved as part of the Word of God: Colossians, Ephesians, Philemon, and Philippians. While some of Paul's letters addressed a particular local need, others were intended to deal with a situation that existed in the churches in the Roman province of Asia. Into the local assemblies had come false teachers with clever arguments to lead the saints away from the truth and back into spiritual darkness. This had happened at Colossae and it was happening at Ephesus. Concerned with the reports he was receiving, Paul wrote to remind the believers that "all doctrine is practical and all practice is doctrinal." What a person believes affects how they live; and how a person lives affects what is believed. Because this is true, Paul will focus attention *first* on the great doctrines of the Christian faith (chs. 1–3) and *then* make practical application (chs. 4–6).

What the believers at Ephesus learned, all Christians must learn. In fact, it is interesting that only in certain ancient manuscripts is the letter addressed "to the saints which are at Ephesus." Some ancient manuscripts omit the words "at Ephesus." It is possible that this epistle was not addressed only to the church at Ephesus, but to all the churches of the province of Asia. It may be that Tychicus had been instructed to take this letter first to Ephesus and then to the other assemblies which included the church at Laodicea. If this is true, then Colossians 4:16 is more clearly understood. There, Paul exhorts the Colossians to read two letters. "And when this epistle is read among you, cause that it be read also in the church of the Laodiceans; and that ye likewise read the epistle from Laodicea." The letter to Laodicea may have been identical to *The Epistle of Paul the Apostle to the Ephesians.*

Overview of Ephesians

Union Obtained (1—3)

The letter itself begins with a salutation (1:1–2), followed by thanksgiving and praise (1:3–23). Not only is Paul thankful for the love and faith of the believers, he is grateful to God the Father for His great mercy in revealing the "mystery" or purpose of His Son Jesus Christ (1:9–12). Chapters one and two form an unbroken *magnificat* in which Paul glorifies Christ in all His riches on behalf of the true saint. Many promises here deserve memorization.

God has saved souls in order that they "should be to the praise of His glory" (1:12). The wise and eternal plan (1:4) of the omnipotent God (1:11) includes a Divine election of souls to salvation (1:4), their sanctification (1:4), predestination (1:5), and adoption (1:5). For all eternity, those who are the heirs of salvation shall give praise to God for their redemption and forgiveness of sin. What a privilege and joy to be part of the Lord's own possessions (1:14), sealed forever with the Holy Spirit of promise (1:13). Herein is true glory.

Herein also are two of Paul's prayers for the saints (1:16–23 and 3:14–21). These deserve study for what we learn about the true heart of one who is walking with Christ: what occupies his thoughts and prayers.

As the glory of God is magnified by the saving of souls, it is further expressed by the unity that exists in Christ among converted Jews and Gentiles throughout the world. There are not two churches, one Jewish and one Gentile. There is only one true Church, for in Christ there is wholeness and harmony (chs. 2–3).

Historically, the Jews had claimed to have almost an exclusive relationship with God because they were His "chosen" people, and because certain promises had been made to Abraham. Now Paul reveals that a new understanding must be embraced. The promises made to Abraham were given on the basis of faith. Abraham believed in God and it was credited to his account for righteousness. All those who have the same faith that Abraham had, whether Jew or Gentile, will share his privileges (cp. Gal. 3:29). But there must be *faith*.

Unity Maintained (4—6)

The doctrine of true saving faith will reveal itself in a life of delightful duty. Those who are called to salvation are called to "walk worthy of the vocation" to which they have been called (4:1—6:20). The saints are not to stay angry (4:26). They are not to steal (4:28). They must show respect to each other, for the Church is a living organism, not a complex organization without feelings. Fornication or promiscuous sexual activity must be stopped (5:3–14). In place of illicit sensuality there should be the singing of songs (5:18–21).

Husbands and wives must love and respect one another (5:22–23). By doing this they will model the relationship that exists between Christ and the Church (5:25, 32). What an incredible picture our God has designed Christian marriage to be! Parents and children are to live in harmony as well (6:1–4). Servants are to honor their masters with faithful service (6:5–9).

Chapter six includes an important passage about spiritual warfare. We face a real enemy who is bent on destroying the Christian's witness and victorious life in Christ. In living out the Christian life, therefore, the whole armor of God is to be used (6:10–20). Truth, righteousness, peace, faith, salvation, the Word, and prayer are the Divine weapons of warfare.

The letter closes with another salutation, a benediction (6:21–24), and a promise that Tychicus, "a beloved brother and faithful minister in the Lord" (6:21) will tell the church specific information about the state of Paul. Tychicus is sent "for the same purpose" (6:22).

14

Joy in Unity

THE EPISTLE OF PAUL TO THE PHILIPPIANS

Written c. A.D. 62
Key word: "Unity"

"For to me to live is Christ, and to die is gain."

—Philippians 1:21

Historical Background

The city of Philippi had a rich history due to its strategic location. Situated on the great Ignatian Highway, it was connected by this Roman road with the important trade routes of the East. The city of Philippi was originally called Krenides, meaning, "The Little Fountains." Philip II, the father of Alexander the Great, became king of Macedonia by force in 359 B.C. and needed financial resources. With the gold from the nearby Krenides region, Philip was able to finance his army for future military conquests. Time passed. The gold mines were depleted and the city of Philippi, renamed after the king, was reduced to a small settlement. In 146 B.C., Macedonia became one of the six provinces governed by Rome. However, the city of Philippi was destined to become important once again because of a famous conflict that occurred there in 42 B.C. It was in that year that the historic battle of Philippi took place: Brutus and Cassius allied themselves against Antony and Octavian, avengers of the death of Julius Caesar. After two fierce engagements, Antony and Octavian were victorious. Brutus and Cassius were dead.

Soon after this battle, Philippi was made a Roman colony. Antony decided to leave some of his warriors there. But their services would again be needed, for political unrest in Rome continued. An ultimate leader of the Empire had to be determined. Either Antony or Octavian must reign, but not both.

In 31 B.C., the naval battle of Actium took place. It was here that Octavian defeated his former ally, Antony. Antony had become infatuated with Cleopatra, the Egyptian queen who had also been the mistress of Julius Caesar. Realizing the hopelessness of their situation, Antony and Cleopatra committed suicide. Octavian was now the undisputed ruler of the Roman Empire. In honor of his great victory, he changed his name to Caesar Augustus. As emperor, Augustus decided to be a "gracious" conqueror. He would allow the people of Italy who had opposed him to join the settlers in Philippi, but only after he dispossessed the citizens of their estates.

As a Roman colony, Philippi enjoyed all the special privileges of Roman citizens everywhere, such as freedom from scourging, freedom from arrest (except in extreme cases), and the right to appeal to the emperor. The people of Philippi liked to dress according to Roman style. Each veteran received from the emperor a portion of land to cultivate. The citizens of Philippi were excused from paying taxes and could direct their own affairs.

The Church at Philippi

By understanding these privileges, we can better understand how the church at Philippi was established (Acts 16), and why Paul would make mention of the progress of the gospel among the members of the Praetorian Guard (Phil. 1:13). Friends and family members of the soldiers who lived in Philippi would want to know if others in the city of Rome had come to faith.

As Paul writes to the church, he gives the apostolic injunction that the believers continue to exercise their citizenship in a manner worthy of the gospel of Christ (1:27). For the Christian in Philippi, life could be very difficult despite great personal freedoms (1:27–30). There were still political pressures to endure. For example, because it was a Roman colony, there was the presence of the imperial cult. The temptation came to compliment the emperor with divine titles and honors that belong only to Jesus Christ (2:5–10). Paul said that this must not be allowed to happen. Those in the church must resist the worship of the emperor without fear (1:28).

Acts 16 records the establishment of the church at Philippi. During his Second Missionary Journey (A.D. 50–54), Paul, accompanied by Silas and Timothy, traveled to the city of Troas. There Paul had a vision in the night (Acts 16:9) of a man inviting him to come and preach the gospel in Macedonia. Being obedient to the heavenly vision, Paul and his party traveled to Neapolis, the port of Philippi. From Neapolis the missionary group proceeded on foot to Philippi, where they would spend their first Sabbath in Europe.

There is a river near the city of Philippi called the Gangites. Somewhere along the river bank, a place of prayer had been established. In the little group assembled was a woman named Lydia. Her home town was Thyatira (now Akhisar, Turkey). We learn a lot about Lydia: she was a seller of purple dye and therefore of considerable wealth; she worshipped God, having been converted from her pagan practices; she listened to the gospel and had her heart opened by the Lord.

Here once more is the ultimate truth that salvation is of the Lord. God must open a person's heart to let the gospel light shine in. Apart from Divine intervention, the heart of the natural man will remain closed to the gospel. It may be refined, cultured, educated, and religious, but the natural heart can only be *renewed* by God. Lydia was converted, and became obedient to gospel duties. She was baptized without delay (16:15). Lydia was a soul winner. Not only did she believe the gospel, but she exposed her household to the message of salvation as well, and they believed. Lydia was grateful to the Apostle Paul; she ministered to them. And she was gracious—she shared what was hers with the other people of God.

"What Must I Do To Be Saved?"

Associated with the founding of the church in Philippi is the conversion of the Philippian jailer. The narrative of this dramatic conversion began the day Paul cast a demonic spirit (Acts 16:16) out of a slave girl who was being used by men to make money because of her ability to make predictions. Paul did not want the gospel message being associated with Beelzebub, a demonic pagan god. When the girl began to follow the missionary group, the Apostle had had enough for the girl was proclaiming, "These men are servants of the Most High God who proclaim to you the way of salvation." What the girl said was true, but everyone knew she was demon possessed. The message was associated with the messenger—and was being rejected! In the name of Christ, Paul cast out the demon that possessed the girl. That is when the real trouble began—for the slave-girl's owners had Paul and Silas arrested. Despite being Roman citizens, they were scourged, publicly disgraced, lied about, and imprisoned, and all this without a trial!

Still, in the providence of God, this injustice was going to work for His own glory; for while in prison Paul and Silas ministered to all who came under the sound of their voices. They sang songs and gave praises to the Lord. Suddenly, God shook the earth, threw open the prison doors, and caused the chains which bound the prisoners to fall off. The men could leave at will!

When the keeper of the prison saw what was happening, he knew that his life would be forfeited if the prisoners escaped (Acts 12:19). Rather than suffer public pain he would take his own life. Drawing his sword, he was about to perish when Paul called out to him to stop. "The prisoners are all here," said Paul. The jailer could not believe it was true. "What must I do to be saved?" he cried. This is the position God wants every sinner to come to: the end of oneself, laying aside all ideas for personal achievement, works, and self-effort, depending upon God alone. Paul gives the clear command for salvation to all repentant sinners: "Believe on the Lord Jesus Christ, and thou shalt be saved!" (Acts 16:31).

The next day the officials of the city sent word to release Paul and Silas. It was then that they found out, to their distress, that they had committed a serious offense against fellow Roman citizens. Had Paul and Silas wanted to press charges, the officials and all who were involved in the beatings could have been in serious trouble. But Paul and Silas were gracious. They soon departed the city as requested, grateful that a church had been firmly established and many souls had found the Savior (Acts 16:40).

Why Written: Joy and Unity

In light of these things, it is easy to see why the church at Philippi was very special to the heart of Paul. Those who came to faith under his ministry in this European city appreciated his labors of love. To show their appreciation, the church sent Paul money. Twice he had received financial support while he was in Thessalonica (Phil. 4:16), again when he was at Corinth (2 Cor. 11:9), and now while still a prisoner at Rome (Phil. 4:18). Paul writes to thank the church for sending their support which had been brought by Epaphroditus.

After bringing the financial gift, Epaphroditus had remained in Rome as a brother and fellow worker. During this period, he grew ill but then recovered (2:25–30). Now he will return to Philippi with Paul's letter and his own restored health. Paul himself hoped to be freed soon (2:19–24). He thought that his case before Emperor Nero would be heard shortly, and his imprisonment would be ended. It is not surprising that *joy* becomes an important theme of this epistle (1:4).

And so it was that in a contented state of mind, Paul wrote an encouraging letter filled with love, hope, counsel, and happiness. He exhorted the believers to "rejoice in the Lord" (3:1) while watching out for false teachers (3:2), especially the Judaizers. He emphasized their need for Christian unity in the midst of these false teachers and temptations toward pride.

Overview of Philippians

Joy in Suffering (Ch. 1)

Paul begins by showing great affection for the Philippians, calling them "partakers" and longing for their "fellowship." His prayer for them (1:9–11) again shows the apostle's heart of love for them—a model for all believers toward one another. And he sites himself as an example of how God uses suffering for good: his chains have allowed a gospel witness even among the Roman prison guards, and have led to boldness among other brethren. Most importantly, Christ is upheld as *our life*—nothing in the world should be allowed to displace our heart communion with Christ.

Joy in Unity (Ch. 2)

Here we have the great biblical principle presented so clearly—that oneness with Christ and with each other depends upon selfless humility, the removal of all pride. The passage in 2:5–11 deserves our careful meditation and is called the *Kinosis*, taken from the Greek word translated "made Himself of no reputation" in 2:7. Christ Himself becomes our great example of humility and obedience.

Joy in the Lord (Ch. 3)

Paul uses himself as an example against the Judaizers, showing that external performance has no place as a motivation for earning favor with

God or man. Our motivation must be in love "that I may know Him" (3:10).

Joy Always (Ch. 4)

Here Paul exhorts the believers to allow their minds to be occupied only with things which are virtuous (4:8), and then concludes with a general benediction (4:20–23). There is here again the great theme of finding our life in Christ alone: "I have learned in whatsoever state I am, therewith to be content" (4:11), and "I can do all things through Christ, which strengthenest me" (4:13).

15

Complete in Christ

THE EPISTLE OF PAUL TO THE COLOSSIANS

Written c. A.D. 61
Key word: "Complete"

"For in Him dwelleth all the fullness of the Godhead bodily. And ye are complete in Him, which is the Head of all principality and power."

—Colossians 2:9–10

Why Written: Exalting the Sufficiency of Christ

During the days of his first imprisonment at Rome, Paul wrote at least four letters which have become part of the canon of Scripture: Colossians, Ephesians, Philemon, and Philippians. Of these four letters, Colossians, Ephesians, and Philemon were written at the same time and delivered by the same people (including Tychicus and Onesimus, Col. 4:7-9; cp. Eph. 6:21). They were sent to the various churches in the province of Asia Minor (the peninsula forming the western section of Asia between the Black Sea on the north, the Mediterranean Sea on the south, and the Aegean Sea on the west). Colossae itself was about 100 miles east of Ephesus. The church at Colossae had not been established by Paul (cp. 2:1) but by Epaphras. Epaphras was a convert of Paul who came to faith while the apostle was laboring for three years at Ephesus (during his Third Missionary Journey, study Col. 1:7; 4:12–13). In fact, it is likely that Paul had never visited Colossae.

The motive for the writing of the letter to the Colossians was a visit to Paul in prison by Epaphras. Epaphras was concerned about Jewish teachers trying to mingle the works of the Law with the grace of the gospel (2:11, 16). Six years earlier, this same false teaching had caused disruption for the Galatians. Now the Judiazers had found fertile soil in Colossae. With the demand to keep the ceremonial law, stress was being laid on the importance of observing special days such as the Sabbath, the new moon, and the feast days. Rules and regulations had been imposed on food and drink. Once more the all sufficiency of Christ for salvation was being undermined—and now with a subtle distortion: to Jewish legalism was added the Greek doctrine of "self abasement and worship of angels" (2:18). This early heresy had entered into the church under the pretext of philosophy (2:8), and later came to be known as *Gnosticism* (lit.: *knowledge*).

Gnosticism was an especially dangerous heresy. It held that knowledge of salvation was given only to those who had received a mystical inner insight. Because sin is done through the physical body, all matter was considered evil. They came to think that they could indulge in sin in the body because it was separate from their inner spiritual goodness. Gnostics also believed that there were different levels of spirits, and that Jesus Christ was one of many lower level messengers who imparted spiritual knowledge. Paul writes to the Colossians to warn of this teaching as heresy (2:16–18). He exalts Christ to them as God incarnate with all the fullness of Deity, being all-sufficient for man's salvation and sanctification.

Overview of Colossians

Pre-eminence of Christ (Ch. 1)

With precise words, after giving a usual salutation (1:1–2) followed by thanksgiving and praise (1:3), the Apostle Paul challenges the believers to hold fast to Christ as the all-sufficient Savior of the soul. The sufficiency of Christ is manifested in the fact that He is very God of very God (1:15–17). He is also the Head of the Church (1:18–19) and the Beginning of the New Creation (1:18b–19). His work of reconciliation has brought peace between God and man (1:20–23), thereby accomplishing the great purpose of Calvary, which is to present the believer holy and faultless before God (1:22; cf. Eph. 5:27). The glory of Christ is manifested by the sufferings Paul endured (1:24–25) and by the gospel which was preached (1:25–29). Though the gospel is a great mystery (1:26), it is now clearly revealed (1:26b). The riches of God's glory are displayed, part of which is the salvation of the Gentiles (1:27b).

In chapter one, Paul again offers a significant prayer for the saints (1:9–12). This reflects and completes his three other prayers in Scripture (Eph. 1:16–19; 3:14–19; Phil. 1:9–11).

Position of the Church (Ch. 2)

Paul continues to show that in Christ "dwelleth all the fullness of the Godhead bodily" (2:9), a direct affirmation of Christ's incarnation as Deity. Therefore, believers are "complete in Him" (2:10). The Church has her identity and function centered in Christ.

Practice of the Church (3—4)

As in other of his letters, Paul follows the prior section devoted to doctrine with a strong exhortation to unite the duties of the new life with the doctrinal truths. The Apostle presents in chapter three a beautiful pattern for believers in every generation: setting our minds on Christ, not on the world (3:1), putting off sin (3:8), putting on Christ (3:10), and then practicing Christlikeness in our relations with one another. The epistle concludes with a final salutation and personal messages (4:7–18).

Four House Churches in the New Testament:

The home of Nymphas in Laodicea	Col. 4:15
The home of Philemon in Colossae	Phil. 2
The home of Gaius in Corinth	Rom. 16:23
The home of Aquila & Priscilla in Rome	Rom. 16:5; 1 Cor. 16:19

The Deity of Christ in Colossians

From Colossians 1:15–20 and 2:9–10, the following facts are stated about Jesus Christ.

(1) the Image of the invisible God;
(2) the First-born of all creation;
(3) all things created through Him;
(4) before all things;
(5) in Him all things consist (i.e., hold together);
(6) head of the body, the Church;
(7) the Beginning;
(8) the First-born from the dead;
(9) in Him all fullness dwells;
(10) through Him all things are reconciled;
(11) Christ in you is the hope of glory;
(12) in Him are all the treasures of wisdom and knowledge;
(13) in Him dwells all the fullness of the Godhead bodily;
(14) in Him the believer is complete (lit. "brought to perfection");
(15) the head of all principality and power.

16

The Second Coming

THE FIRST EPISTLE OF PAUL TO THE THESSALONIANS

Written c. A.D. 51
Key phrase: "Second Coming"

"For they themselves shew of us what manner of entering in we had unto you, and how ye turned to God from idols to serve the living and true God; And to wait for his Son from heaven, whom he raised from the dead, even Jesus, which delivered us from the wrath to come."

—1 Thessalonians 1:9–10

Why Written: Questions of Concern

During his Second Missionary Journey (A.D. 51–54), Paul's burning desire was to go to the city of Ephesus in Asia Minor. Prohibited by the Holy Spirit (Acts 16:7), Paul traveled across the Aegean Sea into Macedonia to Philippi. About six months later, Paul, and those who traveled with him, continued their journey to Thessalonica, the second and largest city of Macedonia. Within four months' time a church was established (Acts 17:1–9). Though the missionary travels continued 50 miles farther west to Berea, Paul manifested true pastoral concern for the newly established church. In time, he would send Timothy back to Thessalonica to see how things were progressing.

Timothy brought back a favorable report on the situation. Despite persecution by unbelieving Jews, the believers were enduring the attacks on their faith. However, they had two particular areas of concern: (1) some had attacked Paul personally, and (2) there were questions about the second coming of Christ. Would it be soon? Would it be sudden and unexpected? If Christ were coming again soon, what about those who had already died? Were there any signs to which people could point, that would indicate the return of Christ was near? Perhaps Paul could explain the situation.

Overview of 1 Thessalonians

Paul's Coming to Them (1—3)

Paul responds to the personal attacks against him with gracious charity and patience. In chapter one, he expresses his love for them. In chapter two, he reviews his ministry among them: it was without impure motives, gentle as a mother, exhorting as a father. This description of Paul's approach to them is a model for any pastor or missionary today.

The Second Coming of Christ (4—5)

It is interesting that the concerns and questions of the saints two thousand years ago have not changed with the passing of time. Christians still ask these same basic questions, and the Church still has the same basic answers, for the Word of God does not change. The truth is this: Jesus is coming again. His return may not be *imminent,* but it is *impending* (study Matt. 25:1–46 and observe the time delay which is emphasized). No one knows the day or hour of the Lord's return, *nor does anyone know the year, generation, or even century* in which Christ shall come again (Matt. 25:13). The believer is not to speculate on this matter, but is simply to be watchful and ready. The Lord will come suddenly like a thief in the night, when He is not expected by the many (1 Thess. 5:1–4). Those who have "fallen asleep" [and who is afraid to go to sleep? For when we sleep we always awake. Note Matt. 27:52; John 11:11; Acts 7:60; 13:36; 1 Cor. 15:6, 18, 20, 51; 2 Pet. 3:4] in Christ will enjoy the initial display of God's omnipotent power at the Lord's glorious Second Coming, for "the dead in Christ shall rise first" (1 Thess. 4:16).

Other wonderful things happen. When the Second Coming takes place, the mortal bodies of the saints who are living shall be changed, "in a moment, in the twinkling of an eye" (1 Cor. 15:51–52). With this glorified body, Christians shall be able to rise to meet the Lord in the air (1 Thess. 4:17). The Dispensational Pre-millennial view of the end times calls this the *Rapture* of the Church, preceding a literal seven year tribulation. The Post-millennial and Amillennial views of the end times see this as a straight-forward description of the Lord's Second (and final) Coming at the final judgment: the Church rises to meet Christ in the air in order to escort the coming King of kings and Lord of lords to His intended destination on Earth, Mount Olivet in Jerusalem (cp. Acts 1:11).

While Christians wait for the Blessed Hope of the Second Coming of Christ, they are to maintain good works and lead a holy life (4:1–8). Together with loving one another, these are the distinguishing marks of true believers during this time. The epistle closes with a number of apostolic exhortations (5:6–28).

Events That Have to Be Fulfilled Prior to the Second Coming of Christ

Prediction	Scripture	Fulfillment
(1) The destruction of Jerusalem	Matt. 24; Mark 13; Luke 21	A.D. 70
(2) Preaching the gospel to the world	Matt. 28:19–20	Acts 2:5; Col. 1:16, 23
(3) The death of Peter by crucifixion	John 21:18–19	c. A.D. 67/68
(4) A long life for the Apostle John	John 21:20–23	died after A.D. 90
(5) The death of Paul	2 Tim. 4:6–7	beheaded
(6) Jesus going to heaven	John 20:17	Acts 1:9
(7) The coming of the Holy Spirit	John 14:16–26	Acts 2:1–4
(8) The suffering of the Church	Acts 14:22	last 2,000 years
(9) The falling away	2 Thess. 2:3	Gal. 1:6
(10) The revelation of an anti-Christ	2 Thess. 2:3	1 Cor. 8:5; cp. Rev. 13:2–18; 1 John 2:22

17

Judgment to Come

THE SECOND EPISTLE OF PAUL
TO THE THESSALONIANS

Written late A.D. 51 or early A.D. 52
Key word: "Judgment"

"And to you who are troubled rest with us, when the Lord Jesus shall be revealed from heaven with His mighty angels, In flaming fire taking vengeance on them that know not God, and that obey not the gospel of our Lord."

—2 Thessalonians 1:7–8

Why Written: Correction of Confusion

When Paul sent his first epistle to the Thessalonians from the city of Corinth, he thought he had answered their questions concerning the Second Coming of Christ. However, new concerns had arisen for two main reasons. First, Paul's teachings in the first letter had been misunderstood. Second, an erroneous teaching had been seriously considered: that the Lord had already come (2 Thess. 2:2). Some interpreted the severe persecution which the church was suffering as the judgmental wrath of God! Once more Paul will minister to the assembly by sharing specific doctrinal truths designed to lead to a practical life of holiness.

Rather than a fear of wrath, their suffering was to produce in them a confident boldness in the Lord to continue their witness for Him.

Overview of 2 Thessalonians

Waiting (Ch. 1)

Paul expresses extensive greeting and comfort, and his great joy "for your patience and faith in all your persecutions and tribulations that ye endure" (2 Thess. 1:4).

Watching (Ch. 2)

Paul points out that the Second Coming of Christ could not have occurred because there had not been a falling away from the faith, nor the revelation of the son of perdition (2 Thess. 2:3). Furthermore, when the Lord does come, He will righteously judge those who have dared to hurt His people (1:7–10). Chapter two contains a description of this day known as the *Day of the Lord*.

Working (Ch. 3)

Since the Lord had not returned according to promise in His glorified resurrected body, the Christian community must continue to work and wait in faith as a vital witness to the world. Those who stubbornly refuse to work must be avoided. If a man will not engage in honest labor, he should not eat (3:10). Paul himself set the example of not being idle nor taking advantage of the goodness of God's people (3:8). The epistle closes with a desire for peace and grace among the people. The letter is declared to be authenticated with a personal signature (3:16–18).

18

Protect the Gospel

The First Epistle of Paul to Timothy

Written c. A.D. 65 or 66
Key phrase: "Protect the Gospel"

"These things write I unto thee, hoping to come unto thee shortly: But if I tarry long, that thou mayest know how thou oughtest to behave thyself in the house of God, which is the Church of the living God, the pillar and ground of the truth."

—1 Timothy 3:14–15

The Tenderness of Timothy

While there are segments in the life of Paul which cannot be documented with certainty, it is probable that after two years of house arrest (Acts 28:30), Paul finally had his trial before the Roman Emperor Nero to whom he had appealed his case when taken into custody in Jerusalem (cp. Acts 21:26–34). Being found innocent of the charges against him from his Jewish accusers, Paul was released about A.D. 63. He immediately resumed his missionary endeavors before he was re-arrested and brought back to Rome, where he was executed c. A.D. 67/68. What is certain is that after his first Roman imprisonment Paul did re-visit the churches he had helped to establish in Macedonia (1 Tim. 1:3). Traveling with him at this time were Titus (Titus 1:5), Luke, and Timothy.

Timothy was a native of Lystra, in the province of Galatia. He was the son of Eunice and the grandson of Lois, both devout Christians. His father was a Greek. From childhood, Timothy had been exposed to those teachings which lead to salvation. It was only natural that his heart was open to being a traveling companion with Paul, and to the work of the ministry during the apostle's Second and Third Missionary Journeys.

Timothy was present with Paul during the First Roman Imprisonment when Colossians, Ephesians, Philemon and Philippians were written (A.D. 61–63) and circulated. Writing to the church at Philippi, Paul says of Timothy that, "I have no man like-minded, who will naturally care for your state" (Phil. 2:20).

Why Written: Pastoral Principles

During the trip through Macedonia, Paul left Timothy at Ephesus to lead the church there (cf. Acts 20:1–3). Timothy soon discovered how difficult the work of the ministry really is. A true church is characterized by order, sound doctrine, and ecclesiastical discipline. But administering these things is not easy. Timothy desperately needed the strength and courage of Paul. To assist and encourage Timothy, the Apostle wrote this letter from Macedonia with practical instructions regarding how to behave as a pastor, in order to put this church in vital spiritual condition so that it could withstand the troubles ahead.

Timothy had a true pastor's heart, a sensitive heart. While sensitivity is a qualification for spiritual leadership, it also means that the attitudes and actions of others are deeply felt. When individuals act well, there is deep appreciation; when others act contrary to sound doctrine, the heart is wounded.

Overview of 1 Timothy

Principles for the Church (1—3)

Paul begins right away to exhort Timothy: stand firm against false teachers; lean on the Lord for strength as the Lord had demonstrated in Paul (ch. 1). Prayer is to form a vital part of the ministry (2:1–3); the conduct of women in the church is described. Paul stressed the quality and qualifications of those people whom Timothy was to allow to help him in leadership roles in the church, namely *elders* (bishops, overseers; 3:1–7) who are to be spiritual shepherds, and *deacons* (3:8–13) who are to support the elders in the ministry.

Principles for the Pastor (4—6)

Other instruction is given concerning false teachers and false doctrine which has its origin in *demonism* (4:1–10), the place of widows in the assembly (5:1–16), the true form of worship, the need for a "called" and specialized ministry (5:17–22), and the role of servants in society (6:1–2). Special warnings are given to those who would be men of integrity in church leadership (6:11–16), and to the wealthy (6:17–19). The letter concludes with a word of exhortation for Timothy not to lose faith, but to "keep that which is committed to thy trust" (6:20).

19

Preach the Gospel

THE SECOND EPISTLE OF PAUL TO TIMOTHY

Written c. A.D. 67
Key phrase: "Preach the Gospel"

"Preach the Word; be instant in season, out of season; reprove, rebuke, exhort with all longsuffering and doctrine."

—2 Timothy 4:2

Why Written: Last Words

This short "pastoral" epistle (the others are 1 Timothy and Titus) is the last of the surviving Pauline letters. It may be the last letter Paul wrote. Shortly after communicating with Timothy, Paul was brought to trial and executed. He had been arrested, perhaps at Troas (2 Tim. 4:13), and taken in chains to a Roman dungeon. Titus had escaped imprisonment and went on to Dalmatia. Now in custody, Paul was left alone with the exception of one faithful friend, Luke (4:11). Not without human emotions, the Apostle was realistic about the fragile future (4:6), realizing from a human standpoint that Christianity might seem on the verge of extinction. Yet he was filled with great faith (1:12–14). He longed for his closest friends to come and be with him (4:9). He knew the great ordeal that he faced. "At my first answer [defense]," he writes, "no man stood with me, but all *men* forsook me" (4:16). "Notwithstanding the Lord stood with me and strengthened me" (4:17).

> Not long afterward the executioner's ax released Paul's soul from his worn and broken body to be borne away by flights of angels to the bosom of his beloved Lord. We imagine his welcome home to heaven surpassed any triumphal procession he had ever witnessed in Rome to returning conquerors. Our guess is that when he got to heaven, his very first act, after a rendezvous with the Lord, was to hunt up Stephen to beg his forgiveness. (Henry H. Halley)

Overview of 2 Timothy

Last Remembrances (Ch. 1)

Paul wants Timothy to stand with him in his final hour. He remembers how they met and how Timothy came to faith. He speaks of Timothy's righteous mother and grandmother and gives thanks to the Lord (1:3–18). The Church can only hope that Timothy and John Mark were able to rush to Rome to join Luke in being with Paul during the final days of his life.

Last Suffering (Ch. 2)

Despite the difficulty of the days, to the very end Paul never stopped being true to his calling as an apostle of the Lord Jesus Christ. He describes his suffering as useful in the hands of a sovereign Lord, and he provides regulations for the life of a minister. A minister is to be strong in the Lord and endure suffering as a good soldier of the cross.

Last Days (Ch. 3)

A minister is to live in such a way that he shall never be ashamed. He is always to handle the Word of Truth in a worthy manner, for there are many apostates in the world. The character of an apostle is clearly revealed (3:1–9), and the Word of God is upheld as authoritative.

Last Words (Ch. 4)

Some had rushed to Rome to accuse Paul. There was, for example, Alexander the coppersmith (4:14). This is probably the same Alexander of Ephesus whom Paul had delivered unto Satan (1 Tim. 1:20). Now, Alexander had a chance to retaliate and so he did Paul "much evil" by testifying against him.

The Apostle's final exhortation to Timothy is to preach the word. He is to preach constantly. "Preach the word: be instant [ready] in season, out of season; reprove, rebuke, exhort [advise] with all long-suffering and doctrine. For the time will come when they will not endure sound doctrine" (4:2–3a). May the Lord grant that all His ministers might be found faithful even unto death.

20

Teach the Gospel

THE EPISTLE OF PAUL TO TITUS

Written c. A.D. 65–67
Key phrase: "Teach the Gospel"

"Teaching us that, denying ungodliness and worldly lusts, we should live soberly, righteously, and godly, in this present world."

—Titus 2:12

Why Written: The Training of Titus

Following his release from his first Roman imprisonment (c. A.D. 63/64), and prior to his second period of incarceration (c. A.D. 66/67), the Apostle Paul wrote two letters: First Timothy and Titus. Titus was a Greek convert who may have been a native of Antioch in Syria. Titus initially appears in the story of the early Church in connection with the Jerusalem Council (A.D. 50). Luke does not record this fact, but Paul does in Galatians 2:3–5.

Titus became Paul's traveling companion during the Third Missionary Journey (A.D. 54–58). He was with Paul at Ephesus before being sent on to Corinth to deal with the difficult situation there. Titus was able to suppress the disruptive behavior that had broken out in the church in that city of pagan culture.

The activities of Titus following Corinth are unknown. He next appears in the biblical narrative c. A.D. 65 on the island of Crete. His ministry in Crete is identified when Paul writes, "For this cause left I thee in Crete, that thou shouldest set in order the things that are wanting, and ordain elders in every city, as I had appointed thee" (1:5). The implication is that Paul himself had been in Crete, perhaps on his way to Macedonia by way of Ephesus, and he had stopped to discuss with Titus the situation in that church.

Titus was to act as a *bishop* (lit. *episcopoi*, overseer) and bring organization to the local assemblies on the island by selecting appropriate officers and ministers of the gospel. Aware of this need, and of the internal pressure again from Judaizers, Paul sends this letter to encourage Titus: (1) to select qualified leaders, and (2) to ensure devotion in the church to "doing what is good."

Overview of Titus

Who to Be Teachers (Ch. 1)

To guide Titus, Paul sets down the qualifications he should look for in church leaders. "For a bishop [note: same as 'elder'] must be blameless, as the steward of God; not self willed, not soon angry, not given to wine, no striker, not given to filthy lucre; But a lover of hospitality, a lover of good men, sober, just, holy, temperate; holding fast the faithful word as he hath been taught, that he may be able by sound doctrine both to exhort and to convince the gainsayers" (1:7-9). These become a standard for all churches everywhere.

In addition to bringing organizational stability to the church in Crete, Titus was to beware of "the circumcision party," or the Judaizers (1:10–16), who argued for circumcision as a sign of spirituality, and then went on to teach "Jewish fables" (1:14). Paul wanted Titus to curb or muzzle their mouths to silence them, for they were subverting (corrupting or overturning) many of the saints (1:11). Paul goes so far as to quote one of their own prophets, Epimenides, as saying, "Cretans are always liars, evil beasts, slow bellies [lazy, idle gluttons]." The Apostle agrees with that secular assessment (1:13).

What to Teach (Ch. 2)

After challenging false doctrine, Titus was to teach and train various groups of people in the assembly for the work of the ministry. Titus was to teach the older men to be "sober" (composed), "grave" (dignified), "temperate" (sensible and discreet), "sound in faith, in love, in patience" (2:2). In like manner, older women are to be holy in their behavior. They are not to be "false accusers" (lit. *not devils*); they are not to be controlled by the devil, the Accuser. Nor are the women to be given to wine. Rather, they are to be teachers of the younger women (2:3–5).

The young women in the assembly are to listen to the older women and learn from them. They are to be "sober" or serious minded, devoted to their own husbands and children while maintaining a holy life (2:4–5). Finally, the young men are encouraged to be sensible and spiritually mature (2:6). Again, this becomes a firm foundation for local church assemblies today.

Because he was to be a teacher to others, Titus must be a good example in all things (2:7–15). He was to be serious minded, genuine in behavior, and without reproach in his speech (2:7–8). By exhorting Titus to set a godly example, Paul knew that any opponent he might have would be put to shame, having nothing bad to say if the truth were told.

How to Teach (Ch. 3)

Paul then very specifically encourages the local church toward "doing what is good," setting forth the duty of the saints to society (3:1–11). The epistle concludes with a final personal message which reveals Paul's desire to have Artemas or Tychicus assuage Titus of his pastoral duties, so that he could join the Apostle during the winter months at Nicopolis, a city in western Greece on the Adriatic Sea (3:12–15, cp. Acts 20:4).

The last mention of Titus in the Bible is in 2 Tim. 4:10. Apparently, Titus had traveled to Dalmatia, a part of the Roman province of Illyricum (in the Balkan peninsula bordering on the Adriatic), which was as far as Paul was able to travel on his Second Missionary Journey (note Rom. 15:19–20). It is probable that after spending the winter together, Paul was arrested and taken in custody back to Rome. Titus may have traveled with him before leaving Rome for Dalmatia, a place well known for its fierce and independent inhabitants. Augustus Caesar had subdued this area during his reign in A.D. 9. According to tradition, Titus returned to Crete, and died in peace in old age as a bishop there.

21

Grace in Practice

The Epistle of Paul to Philemon

Written A.D. 61
Key word: "Grace"

"If thou count me therefore a partner, receive him as myself."
—Philemon 1:17

Why Written: Reconciliation between Brothers

The epistle to Philemon tells the story of a runaway slave named Onesimus (lit. *profitable*), whose journey took him from the kingdom of darkness into the kingdom of eternal light. Philemon is the shortest of the Pauline epistles (25 verses) and the most personal; it is a tender apostolic intercession made on behalf of this young man sold into bondage.

The letter was probably written during the early part of Paul's first Roman imprisonment (c. A.D. 61) along with Colossians (Col. 4:18; Philem. 1:9). Both letters bear the names of the same greeters (cp. Col. 4:7–17 with Philem. 1:23–25). Both letters were delivered at the same time by Tychicus and Onesimus (Col. 4:7–9 cp. Eph. 6:21–22). The main characters in this story are:

- *Philemon*, a wealthy Christian of Colossae;
- *Apphia* (1:2), most likely the wife of Philemon;
- *Archippus*, may have been the son of Philemon, perhaps a pastor of the assembly;
- *Onesimus*, the converted runaway slave;
- *Timothy*, co-laborer with Paul.

The letter begins with a common salutation. It is addressed to Philemon and to the church which met in his house (1:1–3). Several things are known about Philemon. First, he was a resident of Colossae. Second, he had come to faith under the ministry of Paul. Though there is no biblical evidence for this, it is possible that Philemon heard the gospel while visiting Ephesus during the three years of Paul's stay there (Acts 19). What is certain is that Philemon became a leader in the church at Colossae (a small city in Asia Minor southeast of Laodicea and south of Hierapolis) and that his home became a place for the saints to assemble. Philemon is called by Paul, "our beloved fellow worker." He was a faithful follower of Christ.

Like every servant of the Savior, the character of Philemon was tested. His particular test came in how he would treat one of his servants, Onesimus, who had stolen some money from him and fled to Rome. In the providence of the Lord, the runaway thief came into contact with Paul. The Apostle showed him the way of salvation and sent him back to his master.

Overview of Philemon

Praise of Philemon (1:1–7)

Paul begins with praise for Philemon—for his brotherly love and co-labor in the ministry of the gospel.

Plea for Onesimus (1:8–17)

Only thereafter does Paul make a plea for Onesimus: that Philemon would show great restraint and mercy. And on this point Paul is very forceful. Because Onesimus had repented, made restitution as best he could, and asked forgiveness, he then should be forgiven and received back as a "beloved brother" (1:16).

Pledge to Philemon (1:18–25)

Knowing the heart of Philemon, Paul expresses his confidence that Philemon will do even more than he asks. If there are any financial expenses which Onesimus owes, the Apostle promises to pay for them personally when he comes for a visit. Final greetings conclude the letter.

The Question of Slavery

It has been argued that slavery can be accepted as an institution because the Old Testament made provision for it, and because there is no call in the New Testament to abolish it. But the ethics of the Christian religion have always destroyed every institution of human bondage which treats individuals as property instead of persons. If there is "one God and Father of all" (Eph. 4:6), and if all are debtors to Him (Rom. 3:21–26), then no heart with Christian compassion can view another person as something to be used in a selfish way. In Christ, others must become beloved brothers, with their interests esteemed above our own. In just this manner, Paul wanted Onesimus to become a "beloved brother" to Philemon. While the Bible does not tell how Philemon received back his renegade slave, there is a wonderful tradition that the repentant Onesimus was well-received, given his liberty, and eventually became a bishop in Berea, a city in northern Syria.

22

Drawing Near

THE EPISTLE TO THE HEBREWS

Written c. A.D. 61–68
Key word: "Better"

"And having an High Priest over the house of God; Let us draw near with a true heart in full assurance of faith, having our hearts sprinkled from an evil conscience, and our bodies washed with pure water."

—Hebrews 10:21–22

An Unknown Author

The author of the letter to the Hebrews remains one of the great mysteries of biblical studies. He addresses the relationship of Christ to the Levitical priesthood and the sacrifices of the Temple. Origen (c. A.D. 185–254, a theologian of Alexandria, Egypt) writes, "It is not without reason that the men of old have handed it down as Paul's. But who wrote the Epistle, God only knows certainly." Despite some lingering questions, the Eastern Church has credited *Hebrews* to the Apostle Paul from the first. In the fourth century A.D., the Western Church also conceded to apostolic authorship.

Pauline authorship is supported on the basis of indirect evidence such as the mentioning of Timothy in 13:23. During the last years of Paul's life, Timothy remained a close friend and companion, along with Luke. It was not uncommon for Paul to recognize Timothy in some manner when writing. Timothy is named in the salutations of three (Colossians, Philemon, Philippians) of the four letters written to the churches in the province of Asia during his first Roman imprisonment (A.D. 61–63). In addition, the brilliant depth of the doctrinal content seems to be that of the Apostle (note especially Heb. 13:18–25). If Paul is the author, then it is probable that the *Epistle to the Hebrews* was written prior to the destruction of Jerusalem in A.D. 70, and that it was written from Rome c. A.D. 61–63 (cp. 13:24).

Those who do not accept Paul as the author of Hebrews point out that the content of the letter is addressed to Jewish Christians, in a Jewish environment, against the backdrop of Jewish traditions. Paul himself says that he was primarily the apostle to the Gentiles (2 Tim. 1:11). However, this consideration does not constitute a serious challenge to Pauline authorship. All it says really is that Paul, under the inspiration of the Spirit, had the ability to write to the Jews as well as to the Gentiles. The capacity to communicate to individuals in a diversity of language and style speaks well of the versatility of the author rather than against the person.

It is possible that Paul did want to write to the Jewish community to tell them plainly about the gospel of Jesus Christ. After all, he was imminently qualified to do so, being a "Hebrew of Hebrews," and having trained at the feet of one of the most respected rabbis, Gamaliel. Paul's love for his Jewish brethren is well documented, both by his letter to the Romans (note Rom. 10:1) and by his determined visits to Jerusalem, when he knew full well the dangers that awaited him there (Acts 21:10–15).

Why Written: Superiority of the Savior

Many Jews who had professed faith in Christ continued to participate in the Temple worship in Jerusalem. However, when Nero began turning against the Christians, two things became clear: *Judaism* would continue as a protected religion, but *Christianity* would be persecuted. Christians began to be expelled from all Jewish rites (including the Temple). These professing Jewish Christians were therefore forced to *make a choice:* either (1) to follow Christ completely with whole hearts, making a clean break with Judaism and suffering persecution as Christians, or (2) to forsake Christ and return to Judaism, thereby avoiding persecution. It was for them as it is for us today—there is no middle ground of merely "professing Christianity" without a whole-hearted commitment to Christ.

Having come out from the bondage of Judaism himself, the author did not want to see these others return to it. He earnestly warns them not to let persecution destroy their faith and cause them to go back into Judaism. There is good reason, for the gospel goes well beyond the limitations of Judaism. Following the Law alone leads to eternal judgment (by the works of the law no one can be justified, cp. Rom. 3:20). He explains and exhorts them to continue on with Christ to make their faith sure, because Christ is superior to the Old Testament practices in every way.

Overview of Hebrews

Christ's Superiority as a Person (1—4)

Why should anyone follow Christ, especially these Jewish converts who were considering to turn back to their old ways? The author minces no words. He immediately begins to tell them to continue following Christ because the Person and work of Christ is superior to all else. He is better than angels (1:4–14), prophets, high priests, Moses and all other leaders of Israel (3:1–6). While they gave imperfect revelations of eternal truths,

Christ, as the eternal Son of God, has given the fullest revelation of the way of salvation (1:4). There are many appeals to Old Testament passages supporting the truths set forth.

Five Warnings

The structure of *Hebrews* is built around five bold warnings—strong exhortations regarding the disastrous consequences of turning from Christ. Each warning becomes more urgent and severe. The *first* in 2:1–4 is rather gentle, warning these "professing believers" not to allow themselves to drift away ("let slip") from the faith. Compromise and doubting always begin in small increments. The seeker's responsibility is to vigilantly maintain a steady exposure to God's means of His grace flowing to us: the reading and preaching of His Word, prayer, and corporate worship.

The *second warning* in 3:17—4:16 is the longest, and stronger than before. The reader is told to "harden not your hearts" and "take heed lest there be an evil heart of unbelief." The cause of this unbelief is "the deceitfulness of sin." Let none of us think a little compromise will not lead to doubting God's capability to meet all of our needs in Christ. The exhortation is completed with the focus on "entering into His Sabbath rest," a wonderful description of the rest we have in Christ, both now in our daily walk with Him and in future glory.

Christ's Sacrifice as Our Priest (5—10)

The superiority of Christ is further reflected in the fact that His eternal priesthood, typified in Melchizedek, overshadows the Levitical priesthood which was temporal (4:14—7:28). Christ, as the Great High Priest and Mediator of the New Covenant, always and constantly ministers on behalf of all those who trust in Him (8:1—10:18). In addition, His sacrifice is far superior to theirs, being once for all time rather than needing to be repeated continually.

Here too is the clear fulfillment of the *New Covenant* which God had promised approximately 600 years before (in Jer. 31:33–34). The basis for this New Covenant is the finished work of Jesus Christ on the cross at Calvary (cp. Luke 22:20).

> Behold, the days come, saith the Lord, when I will make a new covenant... For this is the covenant that I will make with the house of Israel after those days, saith the Lord: [1] I will put My laws into their mind, and write them in their hearts; [2] and will be to them a God, and they shall be to Me a people . . . [3] for all shall know Me, from the least to the greatest. [4] For I will be merciful to their unrighteousness, [5] and their sins and their iniquities shall I remember no more (Heb. 8:8–12).

The *third warning* in 5:11—6:20 has created confusion for some. It says "it is impossible for those who . . . were made partakers of the Holy Ghost . . . if they shall fall away, to renew them again unto repentance." The implication is that true believers can lose their salvation if they backslide into sin. But that is not what the Scripture means. Remember, the epistle is addressed to "professing believers" who are considering to turn back. Those who in fact do turn away permanently from Christ show themselves to be unbelievers all along. They have "tasted" of the gospel, but they have not been given new life in Christ. It is like the parable of the ten virgins (Matt. 25:1–13), where the five who were ultimately shut out of the Bridegroom's feast also began with some oil in their lamps (a resemblance of some enlightenment by the Holy Spirit, but not a regenerating work).

The *fourth warning* (10:26–39) is even stronger. To "sin willfully" (by choosing to turn away from continually submitting to Christ) is to "count the blood of the [new] covenant . . . an unholy thing!" It is all or nothing, in the kingdom or out, eternally saved or not; there is no middle ground. Truly, "we have need of patience" to endure present trials until the coming of the Lord.

Christ's Sufficiency as Our Provision (11—13)

Based upon these great doctrinal truths, the author exhorts his Jewish friends to be steadfast during their present trials and tribulations, continuing in faith (11:1–40), hope (12:1–14), and love (13:1–25). They are to endure in their saving faith (10:19—12:29). Sustaining faith is illustrated in chapter 11 as twenty-one specific heroes are mentioned in this great "hall of faith."

The *fifth warning* is the strongest of all (12:15–29). The only alternative to the peace of God (at Mount Zion) is the thunderings and judgments of the Law (at Mount Sinai), "for our God is a consuming fire." Why would anyone remain under such punishment for sin? Reader, flee to Christ and without delay!

The closing verses of this Epistle are filled with many exhortations for godly living (13:1–19), which are followed by a salutation and a benediction (13:20–25). Of particular interest is a change in the last eight verses from the third person to the first person singular (13:18–25). The author has an intense personal desire that his readers, today as then, would draw near to Christ intimately.

* * *

The Temple and the Destruction of Jerusalem

Great faith certainly was needed by the Jerusalem Christians, for greater tribulation was in fact still to come. Jerusalem was to be destroyed according to the prophecy of Christ (Matt. 24; Mark 13; Luke 21). The fateful time began in the summer of A.D. 66 when a Jewish revolt broke out. The Roman army was entrusted to Titus, the son of the general Vespasian who had become emperor. On the day of Passover, A.D. 70, Titus made his presence known before the walls of Jerusalem. He had at his command 30,000 experienced soldiers to oppose a Jewish citizen's army of 24,000. According to Tacitus, 600,000 visitors were trapped inside the Holy City. Titus was so impressed by the beauty of the Temple, he pleaded with the residents to surrender in order to avoid its destruction.

But the zealots could not be reasoned with. Five months later the walls of Jerusalem were broken through, a massive slaughter began, and the Temple was burned. Herod's three massive towers were left at the northwest corner to be a witness of the great obstacle Titus had to overcome in capturing the city. Josephus records that more people within the city were killed by the rebellious zealots than by Titus' soldiers. The only people to escape the massacre were the Christians who had fled to Pella.

Before its destruction, the Temple was one of the great wonders of the ancient world and the center for Jewish worship. The first Temple was erected at the same site by Solomon in the 960s B.C., fulfilling a dream of his father, David. Tradition identifies it as Mount Moriah, where Abraham came to sacrifice Isaac. Solomon's Temple was destroyed by the Babylonians when they took Jerusalem's population into captivity in 587 B.C.

The much smaller Second Temple was completed in 516 B.C. by Zerubbabel, when the Jewish remnant returned to their homeland from Babylon. It was heavily fortified in the following centuries. The Roman general Pompeii besieged it in 63 B.C. for three months in establishing Roman rule, when 12,000 Jews died in the fighting.

Shortly after this, Herod the Great was confirmed by Rome as king of the Jews, and he began an ambitious expansion and beautification project. Herod, an Idumean, wanted to assure himself of a permanent memorial. The expansion was needed to accommodate the tens of thousands of Jews who visited Jerusalem for the annual religious festivals (also bringing Herod increased income). The rebuilding project began in 20 B.C., Herod's 18th year of reign, and took 46 years to complete. Detailed descriptions in Josephus' writings have made it possible to create models of the Temple as it must have appeared at its completion.

The Second Temple played a prominent role in Jesus' ministry and early church history. Jesus visited the Temple several times and predicted its destruction (Matt. 24:2). The early Christians assembled at the Temple for worship (Acts 2:46), and Peter performed a notable miracle there (Acts 3). When returning later to Jerusalem after years of missionary work among the Gentiles, Paul was wrongly accused of bringing Gentiles into the inner court (reserved only for Jews) and was arrested (Acts 22).

23

Faith Proven by Works

THE GENERAL EPISTLE OF JAMES

Written: early date A.D. 45–49; late date after A.D. 55
Key word: "Faith"

"But wilt thou know, O vain man, that faith without works is dead?"
—James 2:20

James "the Just"

Four men in the New Testament bear the name of James. They are James the son of Zebedee and the brother of John, James the son of Alphaeus, James the brother of Jesus, and James the father of the Apostle Jude. [Note: In Luke 6:16 the literal translation should read, "And Judas *of* James," an idiom for, "Judas, *son of* James".] The author of this epistle is James, the eldest brother of our Lord, born to Mary and Joseph following Christ's virgin birth (cp. Matt. 13:55; Mark 6:3).

James became a leader in the early church in Jerusalem (Acts 12:17; 15:13; 21:18; Gal. 1:19; 2:9, 12), which reflects God's sovereign grace because James was not willing to believe that Jesus was the Christ until after the Lord's resurrection (John 7:5). Following His victory over death, Jesus made a special appearance to James. He was justified by faith after believing in the death, burial, and resurrection of Christ (1 Cor. 15:7, cp. 15:3).

The leadership of James over the church in Jerusalem is demonstrated by the fact that other apostles reported to him, such as Peter (Acts 12:17, c. A.D. 44) and Paul (Acts 21:18–19, c. A.D. 57). Also, when the Jerusalem Council met in the year A.D. 50 to discuss the question of Gentile circumcision, it was James who announced the final decision: "Wherefore my sentence [judgment] is, that we trouble not them, which from among the Gentiles are turned to God: But that we write unto them, that they abstain from pollution of idols, and from fornication, and from things strangled, and from blood" (Acts 15:19–20). His counsel pleased the apostles, the elders and the whole church (15:22).

The last reference to James in the Bible is found in Acts 21:18–25 in connection with the final visit of Paul to the City of Peace. It was James who suggested that Paul take the vow of the Nazarite (Heb. *nazir*, meaning "to vow, dedicate, consecrate") in order not to offend the unbelieving Jews prior to going into the Temple, or at least to bear the financial burden of those who did (Acts 21:23f).

James did not just write well. He performed what he proclaimed, which is why he was surnamed by others "the Just." He was a man of good works, including prayer. It is said that James spent so much time on his knees calling upon the Lord that they became hard and callous like the knees of a camel. The wise Christian will meditate on the many wonderful words which are found in this book of practical Christian living.

According to Josephus, the Jewish historian, and Hegesippus, a Christian historian (second century), James became a martyr due to political unrest. There was a Jewish uprising in the period following the death of the Roman governor Festus and before the arrival of the new governor, Albinus, in c. A.D. 62. The story is that Ananias, the High Priest and a Sadducee, was alarmed over the number of converts to Christ. He called James before the Sanhedrin and insisted that James renounce Jesus as the Messiah. When James refused, Ananias took advantage of the absence of Roman authority and ordered the Apostle stoned. While he was being stoned, his sufferings were ended when a man took a club and smashed his head. His last words were those of his Lord, "Father, forgive them, they know not what they do."

The dating of *James* is uncertain. An early date has the letter being written between A.D. 45 and 49. A late date places the epistle in A.D. 55 or later. The only thing that seems certain is that the letter was written when the church in Jerusalem was still the focal point of the Christian community.

Why Written: Content of a Controversy

For several centuries a theological controversy has swirled around the message that is found in this epistle. Martin Luther struggled with its contents. It seemed to him that James is in conflict with Paul over the basis of receiving righteousness in order to be accepted by God. Luther interpreted *James* similarly to the way Roman Catholicism still does: that works as well as faith are necessary for salvation, that our "good works" are a way of paying for our sins and earning God's favor. [Luther recognized this as error, and so discounted *James.*] But Paul in his epistles (see Romans 3)—and the whole Bible as well (see Isaiah 53:6)—points to the shed blood of Christ as the complete payment for our sin. In this way, when a person trusts in Christ alone (faith), God grants Christ's righteousness to him without condition. Salvation is based on faith in the Person and work of the Lord Jesus Christ, who alone is sufficient to save (note 2:1).

So, is there a conflict between Paul and James, between their views of faith and works? In a word, No! After Saul's conversion, there were no persecutions against the Church. Professions of Christ among the Jews were relatively easy. There were, therefore, concerns about half-hearted commitments from those who loved being with the Christians, but who did not have a true love for Christ, and who consequently continued to live like the world. So James strips away the outer facade of mere 'profession' to instruct the Church: true saving faith is proven by a changed life.

Overview of James

The book of *James* is a hard-hitting series of tests to prove the genuineness of one's faith.

Test of Trials (Ch. 1)

All sorts of suffering are used by God to purify our hearts from all the worldly desires which keep us from depending upon Him alone.

Test of Works (Ch. 2)

James stresses that when one is truly saved (by faith alone), then his life will show it by the "good works" that he does. In James we have the *practical application* of a life redeemed by the blood of the Lamb, for the truth of the matter is that "faith without works is dead" (2:20). The Puritans liked to point out that while man is saved by *faith alone*, he is not saved by *that faith which is alone*, for true saving faith always results in good works.

    Evangelical faith is repentant faith. It involves supernatural regeneration when one turns to Christ as Lord. This is evidenced when one turns from sin to Christ: a change of masters takes place (Rom. 6:17–18); a death and a resurrection take place (Gal. 5:24–25). If there are no good works (out of a motive of love and not to earn God's favor) following a profession of faith, then that is evidence that a person is not truly saved (Acts 26:20). There is no such thing as a true Christian who continues to live in a lifestyle that is saturated with the world's values! That is the message of James. Instead, a work of transforming grace is produced which must show itself in a new life, a changed life (2 Cor. 5:17). "Yea, a man may say, Thou hast faith, and I have works: shew me thy faith without thy works, and I will *shew thee my faith by my works*" (Jas. 2:18).

In the *Epistle of James*, saving faith is followed by the manifestation of good works, such as pure religion (1:27), the showing of no partiality (2:1), taming the tongue (3:1–12), taking the place of humility (3:13–18), drawing near to God (4:7), abstaining from sensual activities (5:1–7), and the seeking of the salvation of souls (5:19–20).

Test of Words (Ch. 3)

Real faith is also proven by our words, which stem from the heart. May the Lord be pleased to convict all believers to tame our tongues (and our minds) under the control of the Holy Spirit.

Test of Worldliness (Ch. 4)

Real faith is proven by our response to the attractions of the world. We live a new life where Christ satisfies our hearts, and we need none of the world's entertainments or material things to bring us abiding joy.

Test of Time (Ch. 5)

Real faith perseveres in the Lord over time. Difficulties do not push us away from the Lord, they draw us nearer to Him.

24

Partaking of Christ's Sufferings

THE FIRST EPISTLE OF PETER

Written c. A.D. 66
Key word: "Suffering"

"Beloved, think it not strange concerning the fiery trial which is to try you, . . . But rejoice, inasmuch as ye are partakers of Christ's sufferings; that, when His glory shall be revealed, ye may be glad also with exceeding joy."

—1 Peter 4:12–13

The Perseverance of Peter

It is rather easy for readers of the New Testament to identify with Peter, for he was a man of passion who seemed to be constantly either commended (Matt. 16:17) or condemned for the impulsive things he said and did (cp. Matt. 16:21–23). Peter's personality invites warmth and closeness. He appears to be an individual who was easy to talk to because he would understand the things of the heart. In times of suffering and anguish of soul, Peter would be among the first to be sought out for counsel and comfort. His counsel would not be hypothetical but rooted in reality, for Peter himself knew much sorrow in life. He suffered for

Christ's sake in life through imprisonment and then unto death through crucifixion.

There is an ancient tradition called the *Quo Vadis* ("Where are you going?"). It tells of Peter, having been overcome by the urging of his friends, deciding to save himself from ultimate death by fleeing the city of Rome where he had gone to preach. During the night, Peter had a vision while resting on the Appian Way. In the vision Peter met Jesus who was moving in the opposite direction. "Lord," Peter asked, "whither goest Thou?" Jesus answered, "I am going to be crucified again." Peter understood. He bowed his head in submission and returned to Rome, where he was crucified head downward upon request, not feeling worthy to be crucified in the same manner as the Lord. According to Eusebius, Peter's martyrdom took place in the thirteenth year of the reign of Nero (A.D. 67–68).

While tradition is not always rooted in historical facts, it is certain that Peter did suffer for the cause of Christ. It is also certain that Peter is the author. The early Church universally recognized this; Polycarp quotes selected passages from *First Peter* in his *Epistle to the Philippians* (1:8; 2:11; 3:9), as does Irenaeus in his work *Against Heresies* (IV:9, 2; IV:16, 5; V:7, 2).

Why Written: Suffering of the Saints

The Apostle wrote to the churches in Asia Minor (such as Galatia, Ephesus, and Colossae) which were suffering great persecution. Peter wrote from "Babylon" (1 Pet. 5:13), which is probably a veiled reference to Rome (cp. Rev. 17:5, 18)—the Church tried to be careful when speaking about an oppressive authoritarian government. John Mark was with Peter at this time (5:13).

These were difficult days for the elect (A.D. 64–67). In Rome itself, the persecution was pervasive by the permission of the petulant ruler named Nero. Nero blamed the major fire in Rome in A.D. 65 on the Christians. His example caused the persecution to spread rapidly to all

Christian communities. After 35 years of struggling to exist, the Church now faced yet another period of fiery trials (4:12) worldwide (5:9). The devil had come against the saints as a roaring lion seeking to devour (5:8). To encourage the hearts of the saints, Peter sent Silas (5:12), who had also served with Paul, to the churches with encouragement. The apostolic message was simple. Christians must not think it strange to suffer because Christ also suffered and accomplished great spiritual work. The Lord is the Church's Example. The people of Christ must therefore endure hardships patiently (2:20), and without retaliating in kind (3:9). In the end, God the Father will reward the righteous and judge those who do evil (3:12).

Overview of 1 Peter

1 Peter may be grouped into general sections:

- *Security in Suffering*   chapter 1
- *Submission in Suffering*   chapters 2 and 3
- *Steadfastness in Suffering* chapters 4 and 5.

At all times the suffering saints are to remember several things. First, all suffering has a purpose, though at times it is not easy to discern what that purpose might be (1:6–7; 2:19–20; 3:14; 4:14). Second, suffering is to be expected (4:12). Third, suffering is not to be dreaded or avoided (3:14), but is to be endured patiently (2:23; 3:9), with a measure of rejoicing (4:13). Fourth, the example of Christ is the pattern for how suffering for righteousness sake is to be endured (cp. 1:11, 2:21 and 5:1, with 2:21 and 4:1–2). Fifth, all the suffering that the saints will encounter is according to the will of God (4:19).

25

Knowledge of Our Lord

THE SECOND EPISTLE OF PETER

Written c. A.D. 66–67
Key word: "Knowledge"

"But grow in grace, and in the knowledge of our Lord and Savior Jesus Christ. To Him be glory both now and for ever. Amen."

—2 Peter 3:18

Why Written: Words of Warning

Unlike *First Peter*, this second epistle which bears the name of the leading apostle was not widely received as authentic until the days of Origen (c. A.D. 250). However, there is no reason not to accept this letter as being Petrine and legitimate. The thoughts are orthodox. There are no new teachings, nor is there any departure from the gospel. Furthermore, the autobiographical accounts are consistent with other known facts (1:16–18, cp. Matt. 17:1–9). For example, Peter knew he was going to die a violent death according to the prediction of Christ (cp. John 21:18–19 with 2 Pet. 1:12–14). Finally, the epistle specifically claims Simon Peter as its author.

The recipients of the epistle were the saints of Asia Minor (cp. 1 Pet. 1:1 with 2 Pet. 3:15). Knowing that false teachers would be coming in among those who profess to know the Lord, Peter prepares and warns the general Church to stand firm against them, and to hold fast to the true knowledge of God. It is a warning which is as valid today as it was then.

Overview of 2 Peter

True Knowledge: Explained (Ch. 1)

Distinctive themes may be identified in the *Second Epistle of Peter*, beginning with the Apostle's desire that the believers make sure of their salvation (1:5). This can be done in two basic ways: (1) there must be a partaking of the divine nature by faith (1:4), and (2) the fruit of righteousness must be manifested. Seven divine qualities are listed: virtue, knowledge, self-control, patience, godliness, brotherly kindness, love (1:5–11).

False Knowledge: Exposed (Ch. 2)

As the Apostle wants the saints to be sure of their calling, so he wants the Church to beware of false teaching within the assembly. He warns against apostasy (2:1–22) and speaks of destructive heresies (2:1). False teachers are characterized by covetousness (2:3), sensuality (2:10), ruthlessness (2:12), with eyes full of adultery (2:14). False teachers are servants of corruption (2:19). As horrible as the world can be, the sin found within the holy sanctuary, the church, is even more hideous. There is only one hope for both the secular and sacred: the Second Coming of Christ.

True Knowledge: Effects (Ch. 3)

While some in the early Church may have wanted the Second Advent to take place sooner rather than later, Jesus did teach that His return would be after a long period of time (Matt. 25:19). There is wisdom in preparing for the impending return of Christ (Matt. 25:4), without embracing emotional rhetoric about an imminent return (as if a particular generation can discern the signs of the time better than all others). Those who live in a highly emotional state of belief that theirs is the "terminal generation" are subject to spiritual depression when time moves on and the Lord has not returned according to human expectations. Peter reminds the Church that, "The Lord is not slack concerning His promise, as some men count slackness; but is long-suffering to us-ward, not willing that any should perish, but that all should come to repentance" (3:9). No matter how dark the days of human history may grow, in the end the Lord will deliver His own from ultimate destruction and, for them, there will be a new heaven and a new earth (3:13–14).

In conclusion, Peter speaks of the epistles of Paul (3:15) as being part of the canon of Scripture (3:16). He admits that there are some things hard to understand for the unbelieving. In contrast, the believer can know the full counsel of God and, if the heart is guarded, will not be led away into error. The epistle concludes with the exhortation to "grow in grace, and in the *knowledge* of our Lord and Savior Jesus Christ" (3:18).

26

Fellowship with Christ

The First Epistle of John

Written: early date prior to A.D. 70; late date c. A.D. 80–95
Key word: "Fellowship"

"That which we have seen and heard declare we unto you, that ye also may have fellowship with us: and truly our fellowship is with the Father, and with His Son Jesus Christ."

—1 John 1:3

John: The Son of Zebedee

There are several individuals named John (lit. *God is gracious*) in the New Testament. There is a particular priest named John, who was on the council (before whom Peter and John were brought following the healing of the lame man at the Gate Beautiful, Acts 4:6). There is John Mark who wrote the second Gospel (Acts 12:12, 25; 13:5; 15:37). There is John the son of Zechariah, a priest in the lineage of Abia (Luke 1:5), who is known as John the Baptist. His ministry began shortly before that of Christ, in fulfillment of prophecy (Isa. 40:3; Mal. 3:1). Finally, there is John the son of Zebedee, who became a disciple of

Christ. He is the author of five books of the Bible: the *Gospel of John, 1 John, 2 John, 3 John*, and the *Revelation*.

The date normally attributed to the first Johannine epistle is placed by scholars either as an early date, prior to A.D. 70, or as a later date, between A.D. 80–95. The exact dating of John's epistles is not so important, except when we consider the *Revelation*, because only there does the date of writing affect proper interpretation.

John was in Ephesus when he wrote his epistles, serving as the leader of the church there. He thinks of his people as "my little children" (1 John 2:1), a reference to the circle of Gentile believers in Ephesus (5:21).

Why Written: Falsehood versus Fellowship

Similarly to Paul in his *Epistle to the Colossians*, John's purpose in writing his letters was to combat the rise of *Gnosticism*, the first major heresy in the early churches (see chapter 14). Gnosticism was a mixture of Greek philosophy, Jewish legalism, and Eastern mysticism. It taught: that matter was evil, that God did not create matter, but that an *eon* (a spirit) emanated from God until one of "them" created all things. In Gnosticism, angels were worshipped. The followers of this system came to believe that they were spiritually superior to all others, but yet sexual promiscuity was allowed. A *dualism* was embraced whereby there was a division between the soul and the body: what the body did might be sin, but it did not matter because the soul was pure.

As John wrote to combat the rise of Gnosticism in general, he also wrote to challenge the teaching of Cerenthus in particular. Cerenthus was the first heretic of the early Church. He suggested that the "Christ" was different from "Jesus." The "Christ," he said, was immaterial, sinless, and spiritual perfection. In contrast, "Jesus" was a material, sinful person. The "Christ" came upon "Jesus" at His baptism, but left Him prior to the crucifixion, so that it was the sinful man who died at Calvary.

Once, John fled from a bathhouse to which Cerenthus had come, crying out, "The enemy of the truth is within."

These thoughts deny the *incarnation*, that God became *man*. They also deny that the *God-man* died. It is instructive to notice that the denial of the *humanity* of Christ was challenged at the end of the first century, whereas the denial of the *deity* of Christ is the challenge to the Church in our day. The teaching of Cerenthus led to *Docetism*, which taught that Jesus only *appeared* to be a man. That He only *appeared* to be real, said Docetism, is confirmed by the life He lived, the miracles He worked, and the death He died! Surely "God" could not have endured as this, they said. But John and the entire New Testament prove both the deity and the humanity of Christ.

Overview of 1 John

As John wanted to combat Gnosticism (1:1, 3:9, 5:6), he also wanted to accomplish other objectives. He wanted them to know fellowship with God (1:3) and joy as a Christian (1:4). John will teach that true joy does not come from circumstances, but from communion with Christ and other believers. John also wrote so that the Christians should not sin (2:1). Nor should they be deceived. As an apostle, John was determined that all teachers in the churches be tested for the truth (4:1). Chapters 2 and 3 contain over 25 tests which indicate whether or not a 'professing Christian' is truly saved. Finally, with a pastor's heart, John wanted the true believers to have assurance of their salvation (5:11-13).

The Spirit of Anti-Christ

The primary biblical teaching of anti-Christ is found in the epistles of John, for the word only appears in the writings of this apostle.

Four verses set forth the biblical teaching. Anti-Christ is:

(1) anyone who denies that Jesus is the Christ (1 John 2:22);
(2) anyone who denies the Father and the Son (1 John 2:23);

(3) every spirit that does not confess Jesus (1 John 4:3);

(4) all those who do not acknowledge Jesus Christ as coming in the flesh (2 John 4:7).

27

Walking in Truth

THE SECOND EPISTLE OF JOHN

Written c. A.D. 60–95
Key word: "Truth"

"I rejoiced greatly that I found of thy children walking in truth, as we have received a commandment from the Father."

—2 John 1:4

The Last Companion of Christ

In this short epistle, John introduces himself as the Elder (lit. *Presbyter*) after the pattern of Peter (cp. 1 Pet. 5:1). If this indicates his age and position, then John is probably now alone of all the original disciples. Peter has been crucified; Paul has been beheaded. The other apostles have all suffered martyrdom. John is the elder Christian statesman; he is the last surviving companion of Christ.

His letter is addressed to the "elect lady and her children." It is possible that John has a specific woman in mind. That would not be surprising, for women played a vital role in the early churches. However, it is also possible that John writes in veiled language as a pastor to his people. The Church is considered in feminine terms (note Eph. 5:23–

33). In like manner, the "elect sister" (2 John 1:13) may be another prominent Christian woman in the congregation, or the congregation itself.

Why Written: The Language of Love

No mention is made of the place from which the Apostle writes nor of the church to whom he writes. Stress is placed upon the content of the letter. This includes a message of love and fellowship, while warning against false teachers and their tendency to deceive others. The false teachers (1 John 2:18–29) went from church to church to teach new doctrines in the name of Christ. The custom was to welcome traveling Christians into homes in order to hear news from other churches, to receive more complete teaching, and to encourage one another.

However, these false doctrines are in reality destructive to the Christian faith. John commends the "elect lady" for her hospitality, but exhorts her for a lack of discernment. He wants the Church to be aware of such individuals and refuse them unconditional hospitality. In a time when false teachers were traveling all over the Roman Empire, there was a real need to break fellowship with those who would deny the cardinal doctrines of the faith.

Overview of 2 John

John is careful to explain that this lack of social etiquette does not mean some are to be loved less (1:5–6). It does mean that encouragement and acceptance should not be given to those who are the enemies of the Cross.

The word "truth" is important to John as it was important to Jesus, who said "I am the Truth, the Way, and the Life," and "the Truth shall set you free." John writes of loving those who are in Truth (1:1) and who know the Truth (1:1). He speaks of the Truth which dwells in the saints (1:2), and of grace, mercy, and peace coming in Truth (1:3). John rejoices that the saints are found to be walking in Truth (1:4) or embracing Truth—by which he means the doctrines of Christ. That is important, because anyone who does not abide in the doctrine of Christ "hath not God" (1:9).

28

Hospitality

THE THIRD EPISTLE OF JOHN

Written c. A.D. 60–95
Key word: "Hospitality"

"We therefore ought to receive such, that we might be fellow-helpers to the truth."
—3 John 1:8

Why Written: Separating from Saints

The human author of this epistle is John, the beloved disciple. The Divine Author is God the Holy Spirit (2 Tim. 3:16). According to Eusebius (*Ecclesiastical History*, section 3:25), John returned from being exiled on Patmos to Ephesus following the death of Domitian in A.D. 96. He visited the churches of Asia, preached the gospel, ordained elders, and administered church discipline when necessary. Gaius, the recipient of the letter, may have been a member of one of the seven churches in the Roman province of Asia that John cared for (cp. Rev. 1:4).

In the providence of the Lord, the Apostle Paul was instrumental in establishing churches in and around the city of Ephesus. Soon thereafter, a practical problem arose—finding proper pastoral care. The

Apostle John helped in this area. He gathered around himself individuals to train, and sent them forth to the developing congregations. Unfortunately, among those who went out was a domineering teacher named Diotrephes. It appears that he and Gaius were pastors of separate congregations in the same city.

When the evangelists sent by John came to his assembly, Diotrephes refused to receive them, but Gaius did. Diotrephes was encouraging closed doors to anyone that disagreed with him, even on minor doctrines, in order to maintain a position of power out of a motive of pride. Upon returning to Ephesus, John heard of the shameful way the traveling evangelists had been treated. He sent another delegation to the same city with a letter addressed to Gaius.

The identity of this particular Gaius is uncertain. Several individuals with the same name are known to the Christian community. There was a Gaius [lit. *lord*] who was a native of Macedonia and a companion of Paul. He was attacked by a mob at Ephesus, c. A.D. 54 (Acts 19:29). There was another Gaius who was from Derbe. He too was a companion of Paul when the apostle was returning from Macedonia into Asia (Acts 20:4). It may be that this Gaius was a resident of the city of Corinth whom Paul baptized. Christians assembled in his home (Rom. 16:23; 1 Cor. 1:14). Perhaps this Gaius was the bishop of Pergamos who is spoken of in another early work (*Apostolic Constitutions*, section 7:40).

Overview of 3 John

While John had written 2 John to admonish the extreme of too open hospitality, he now writes Gaius to encourage him that Diotrephes was erring on the opposite extreme: too narrow hospitality. John's message is that we should maintain fellowship with those who are in agreement on the cardinal doctrines, even when there is minor variation in beliefs on other doctrines.

John desires in love that Gaius have physical health and spiritual strength (1:1–4, cf. 1 Thess. 2:19–20). Gaius is commended for his graciousness to others in the community of Christ. In contrast to Gaius, John has some harsh things to say about Diotrephes and his fleshly ambition (1:9). It is possible that Diotrephes was without true saving knowledge (1:11), for he was uncharitable and domineering (1:10). There was nothing in his life to be emulated. Diotrephes should have been more like Demetrius, whose living testimony bore witness to the truth. John has more to say to Gaius, but closes with a desire to see him soon and a gracious benediction.

29

Keep from Falling

The General Epistle of Jude

Written c. A.D. 67
Key word: "Keep"

"Now unto Him that is able to keep you from falling, and to present you faultless before the presence of His glory with exceeding joy."

—Jude 1:24

A Dramatic Distinction

Bible scholars are not united on the identity of the author of this epistle. There is an ancient tradition that the writer was the brother of James, who was also the brother of Christ (Matt. 13:55, Mark 6:3). As the brothers of Jesus, James and Jude were initially skeptical about His messianic claims (John 7:3–5). After the Lord's resurrection, they believed and served Him well. James became a leader of the church in Jerusalem (Acts 1:13, 15:13ff, Gal. 1:19), and the author of the epistle that bears his name (Jas. 1:1). Jude also wrote an epistle to the church, teaching his spiritual children quietly to follow the Savior.

Eusebius of Caesarea (c.260–c.340), an early church historian, records that when the Emperor Domitian (A.D. 81–96) began an official persecution of Christians, he ordered the arrest of the grandsons of Jude. When they appeared before Domitian, they told the Emperor they were humble farmers owning only 39 acres, from which they raised their taxes and supported themselves. They were a threat to no one for Christ's kingdom was not of this world. Domitian dismissed them (*Ecclesiastical History*, section 3:19–20).

Despite the voice of tradition, others believe that this Jude (English), Judas (Latin), or Judah (Hebrew), whose name means "praise" or "celebration," was one of the Twelve Apostles (Luke 6:16; John 14:22). If so, he was called Thaddaeus by Matthew and Mark (Matt. 10:3; Mark 3:18). The reason for the uncertain identity is that the name Jude was quite common. It was given to the best of men (Gen. 29:35) as well as to the worst of men such as Iscariot.

What is certain is that in verse 1, Jude identifies himself as the author of the letter and declares himself to be "the servant of Jesus Christ." For Jude, the title of servant was an honorable one. We are reminded that it takes great dignity to serve others and serve them well with humility.

As Jude was the servant of Christ, he was also "the brother of James." Again, if James refers to the apostle, then we know that the father of these men is spoken of in Scripture as being Alphaeus (Matt. 10:3, Mk. 3:18). What a privilege it must have been for Alphaeus to see his sons find and follow the Messiah, thereby becoming servants of the Son of Righteousness. As a servant, Jude was given the honor of writing part of the Word of God which will live and abide forever.

The Bible is very careful to make a dramatic distinction between the author and Judas Iscariot (cp. John 14:22), for what a difference there was. Whereas one was faithful, the other was faithless. While one confessed Christ, the other betrayed Him. One brought honor to the Lord's name, while the other was a living contradiction of corruption clothed in goodness. According to tradition, Jude was crucified in A.D. 72 at Edessa, Greece.

Why Written: False Teachers

Jude wrote what is considered to be a general epistle. Unlike other letters addressed to a single person (such as Timothy, Titus, and Philemon), or to a particular church (such as the one in Corinth), Jude wrote to the Church of Christ at large. Probably about A.D. 67, not long before the martyrdom of Peter and of Paul at Rome, Jude writes to all who are "sanctified" or "set apart" in Christ Jesus.

One important reason for writing this epistle was to give a word of warning to the saints about false teachers and their false doctrines (Jude 1:8–16). The Church has always had to challenge individuals who want to introduce new concepts that are contrary to the truth given by Christ and about Christ. False teachers constantly threaten the common or general teaching about the Person and work of Christ.

Overview of Jude

Danger (1:1–16)

A militant defense of *the* faith is called for (Jude 1:3b). There is a "faith"—a body of truth that is complete and final. There are no new revelations and truths that can be added to the canon of Scripture. All false teachers can do is to challenge Christ's sovereignty and His lordship (1:4, cp. 2 Pet. 2:1).

Jude writes against false teachers in strong language as he speaks of "certain men crept in unawares, who were before of old ordained to this condemnation, ungodly men, turning the grace of our God into lasciviousness, and denying the only Lord God, and our Lord Jesus Christ." Specific sins are charged to the false teachers. *First*, they fail to remember past judgments of God illustrated by the Israelites in the wilderness (1:5), by the fallen angels (1:6), and by the citizens of Sodom and Gomorrah (1:7). *Second*, they dream filthy dreams for they are spiritually asleep (1:8). *Third*, they defile the flesh with sexual immorality (1:8). *Fourth*, they despise authority including that of God's Word, and speak evil of earthly and heavenly dignitaries (1:8). Not even Michael the archangel was as bold as the false teachers of whom Jude wrote (1:9, cp. 1:10).

Cain, Balaam, Korah

These teachers of falsehood are self-willed, for "they have gone in the way of *Cain*" (Gen. 4:3–8). Cain refers to the strong-willed natural man who rejects the required blood sacrifice. Cain would rather substitute the works of his own hands and have it accepted by God (1:11a). The religious leaders are like that. They will not accept the substitutionary work of Christ but go about to establish their own religion.

Moreover, the false teachers run "greedily after the error of *Balaam*" (1:11, cp. Num. 22—24). The error of Balaam refers to the belief that God must judge all sin apart from any mercy (cp. 2 Pet. 2:15, Rev. 2:14). The greed of Balaam refers to the taking of money for spiritual services apart from truth or justice. All of this is done because of spiritual lawlessness, manifested in the rebellion of *Korah* (cp. Num. 16:1–50, 26:9–11). Korah and his followers denied God's authority expressed through the persons of Moses and Aaron. A rejection of the Word of God is a basic characteristic of all false teachers.

Word Pictures

The spiritual bankruptcy of the false teachers is indicated by the risk they take to destroy others. "These are spots in your feasts of charity," said Jude or literally, "They are hidden rocks" on which the love feasts of the Christians were in danger of being wrecked by selfish, sensual cavorting (cf. 1 Cor. 11:30–32). The spiritual barrenness of the false teachers is like clouds without water and trees without fruit (1:12b). When their roots of righteousness are plucked up and examined, they are visibly seen to be dead.

The shame and deception of the false teachers also reveal a vacuum of spiritual reality (1:13, cp. Isa. 57:20). There is only one end for the false teachers. They shall be destroyed by Christ at His second advent just as Enoch prophesied (1:14–15). The judgment of the false teachers will be just for they are nothing more than "murmurers" (grumblers), "complainers" (malcontents), "walking after their own lust," with mouths speaking great, swelling, boastful words (1:16).

Duty (1:17–25)

The people of God are to remember the apostolic words and love the truth (1:17–18; cp. 1 Tim. 4:1–6, 2 Tim. 3:1–10, 2 Thess. 2:1–12, and 2 Pet. 2:1–22). Spiritual truth can be recognized in that it magnifies the Person and work of Jesus Christ and promotes holiness. Titus 1:1 speaks of *"the truth which is after godliness."* The people of God are to move towards spiritual maturity (1:20a). This is characterized by prayer (1:20b), love (1:21a), a belief in the mercy of God (1:21b), compassion (1:22), soul-winning efforts (1:23a), and a definite separation from sensuality (1:23b). The epistle closes with a wonderful benediction of praise to God for His ability to preserve His own (1:24). The Church has cause to praise the *"only wise God our Savior"* (1:25).

30

Christ is Lord!

The Revelation of Jesus Christ

Written: early date prior to A.D. 70; late date c. A.D. 90–95
Key phrase: "Christ is Lord"

"Allelujah: for the Lord God Omnipotent reigneth!"
—Revelation 19:6

The Last Letter

The last of the letters of the Apostle John is also the last book of the Bible. It is the vision of prophecy of "things which must shortly come to pass" (1:1). Because commentators have not agreed on the meaning of these words in particular, nor upon the message of the *Revelation*, various methods of interpretation have emerged to guide our understanding.

Spiritual. Supporters of the mystical or allegorical interpretation of the *Revelation* find a basic conflict between the Church and the forces of evil until Jesus returns. Christians are to be tested severely for their faith in every generation. Critics of the spiritualization of the *Revelation* argue that this method of interpretation is not rooted in reality, and ignores the prophetic nature of the narrative (cp. 1:3; 10:11; 22:7, 10, 18–19).

It is argued that special attention is not paid to the "interpretive key" to the book (1:19), nor to the great events surrounding the Second Advent (1:7; 3:11; 16:15; 22:7, 12).

Historical. Also known as the "Preterist View," this school of thought argues that most of the *Revelation* has been historically fulfilled, mainly in the devastating judgment upon Jerusalem in A.D. 70 by the Romans. The great themes of the book have been realized by way of interpretation. The False Prophet and the Beast have been destroyed in the defeat of the Jewish enemies of the early Church and in the person of Nero. A key verse for the Preterist View is 1:1, where John is told that he will be shown things that must *shortly* come to pass.

One important factor for deciding which method of interpretation should be embraced is the dating of the *Revelation*. If a late date theory is held (c. A.D. 90), then it is possible that all that John saw is still futuristic. However, if an early date (c. prior to A.D. 70) of the *Revelation* is held, then it is possible that all John saw is now past: Jesus said that "what John saw" would soon happen (cp. Matt. 24; Mark 13; Luke 21), and history records that it did happen in A.D. 70.[1]

---

[1] Students of the Bible examine external and internal evidence to date a particular book. External evidence is the witness of persons and or events outside the Scripture. Internal evidence is the witness of the document itself. The primary external witness for a late date (between A.D. 90 and A.D. 95) is Irenaeus (A.D. 130–202). In fact, Irenaeus is the only source for the late date of the *Revelation*. All other sources (Clement of Alexandria, Origen, Victorinus, and Jerome) simply quoted from him. However, early Christian tradition is far from being of one accord in assigning the Apocalypse to the late date, the last years of the reign of Domitian (A.D. 81–96). There were many voices which taught that the *Revelation* was written under Nero (A.D. 54–68). Furthermore, Irenaeus himself was not always careful in his critical facts, illustrated by his statement that Jesus lived to be fifty (Irenaeus, *Against Heresies*, section 2:25:5)! That the destruction of Jerusalem was indeed seen to be the fulfillment of the Lord's predictions, as set forth in Matthew 24, Mark 13, and Luke 21, is reflected by the following: the writings of Eusebius (*Ecclesiastical History*, Book 3, Chap. 5–8), Origen's commentary on Matthew and *Against Celsus* (2:13), Clementine's *Homilies* which discusses Matthew 24:2–34, and the works of Clement of Alexandria's *Miscellanies*, which discusses Daniel 9:24–27. The simple conclusion is that biblical scholarship is not set aside by favoring an early date.

Successive Ages. A more imaginative method of interpretation of the *Revelation* believes that the history of the Church is set forth in seven successive ages. The *Revelation*, then, is an *outline* of "things to come" (1:1). The chapters are divided so as to represent these seven ages: chapters 1–3, 4–6, 7–11, 12–14, 15–16, 17–19, and 20–21.

While this view has become popular in recent years, one major problem is that it tends to interpret the biblical narrative in light of contemporary events—rather than the other way around, where contemporary events are interpreted by the Bible.

Futuristic. Using 1:19 as a key text, this view of the *Revelation* places most of the book (chap. 4–22) in the future; it is actual prophecy about real future events. Many Old Testament concepts are mingled into this view, including a belief that "the day of the Lord" is also futuristic (cp. Isa. 2:10–22; 4:1–6; 34:1–17; Joel 2), as well as the Lord's kingdom (cp. Isa. 35:1–10). While some of the early Church fathers (such as Justin Martyr, Irenaeus, Hippolytus, Tertullian, and Victorinus) may have held to a literal view of a future kingdom, other theologians such as Augustine challenged their ideas.

Regardless of the view of interpretation, the main message stands clear: Jesus Christ will reign supreme as Lord over all. The *Revelation* reveals to us the personal majesty of Jesus Christ. Therefore, we should look for Jesus in its pages. What we can learn of Him is much more important than what we can learn of the end times.

An Unusual Style of Writing

Another important consideration when interpreting the *Revelation* is the style of writing in which it was written. It is a very specific literary form called "Apocalyptic literature." Several points should be noted [the following is abstracted from William Barclay's *The Daily Bible Study Series, The Revelation of John*, Volume 1].

1. The Greek word *apolalupsis* means literally *"an unveiling."* The purpose of the writer was to *unveil* a particular meaning by using signs and symbols.
2. Apocalyptic literature, as a style of writing, appeared in earnest during the period 210 B.C.–A.D. 200. These were especially dark days in Jewish history, demonstrated by the reign of Antiochus Epiphanes (175–164 B.C.). Later, there would be persecution of Christians under the iron fist of such Roman emperors as Nero and Domitian.
3. These difficult times gave birth to apocalyptic literature. Examples of apocalyptic literature can be found in the Old Testament in Daniel (chap. 7–12); Isaiah (chap. 24–27), Ezekiel (chap. 37–41), and Zechariah (chap. 9–12).
4. As a result of these writings two things happened. First, loyalty to one's nation, family, and spiritual heritage was stressed. Second, faith was encouraged. Jewish society never stopped believing that it was chosen by God and destined to consummate world domination.
5. When the whole history of national Israel challenged these hopes, the Jews turned to a design of history to continue their beliefs. Time was divided into two ages. There is this present age which is completely bad and beyond amends; there is nothing to foresee but total destruction in the Day of the Lord. And there is the age to come which is entirely good, the golden age of God bringing peace, prosperity, and righteousness.
6. Apocalyptic literature has a pattern. Certain themes occur over and over again:

- The Messiah is a divine, eternal figure full of power and glory (Ezra 13:25–26).
- Before the Messiah came, Elijah would return to prepare the way for Him (Mal. 4:5–6).

- The coming of the Messianic Age would be like the agony of birth (Matt. 24:8, Mark 13:8).
- The last days will be a time of universal upheaval (Isa. 13:10; Joel 2:30, 3:15), and great horror (Zeph. 1:14).
- Human relationships will also be destroyed as honor is turned into shame, strength into humiliation, and beauty into ugliness (Zech. 14:13).
- It is a time of judgment as sinners are dealt with (Mal. 3:1–3; Isa. 66:15–16).
- The Gentiles who had subdued Israel had an uncertain destiny:
  - Sometimes the vision was of their total destruction (Isa. 13:19–22, 63:6, 45:14).
  - Sometimes the vision was of the regeneration of the Gentiles (Isa. 49:6, 51:5, 45:20–35).
  - Sometimes the vision was of one last gathering of Gentiles against the Jews at Jerusalem (Ezek. 38:14-39:16, Zech. 14:1–11).
- Jews will be regathered to the Holy City (Isa. 27:12-13).
- The dead will rise (Dan. 12:2–3).
- The Jews were to enjoy a New Jerusalem to replace the old city destroyed by Babylon.
- From the Holy City the Messiah would reign. Some said forever (Dan. 7:27). Others said for only four hundred years (based upon Gen. 15:13, cp. Psa. 90:15).
- All agreed that in the glorious *Age to Come* there would be a united Israel with all the tribes re-gathered (Jer. 3:18; Isa. 11:13; Hos. 1:11). In the *Age to Come*, the world would be fruitful like the Garden of Eden (Isa. 32:15, 35:1, 51:3), all wars would cease (Isa. 2:4), nature would be at peace (Isa. 11:6–9, Hos. 2:18), and there would be no more pain or sorrow (Jer. 31:12; Isa. 35:10, 65:10–22).

The *Book of the Revelation* incorporates most if not all of these majestic themes, but from a significantly different focal point. Sounding forth a prophetic voice, the *Book of the Revelation* radically departs from other works of apocalyptic literature in that it ends with hope. For many, the world is beyond hope. For the Christian, there is a confidence in the faithfulness of God and the redeeming Lordship of Christ!

The Spiritual Significance of Special Numbers

As the *Book of the Revelation* uses a special style of writing, it also uses specific numbers in a symbolic way: four, seven, twelve, and thousand. In the *Revelation* we find *four* living creatures, four horsemen, and four angels. There are *twelve* elders, twelve gates to the city of God, twelve foundations, and twelve varieties of fruit on the tree of life. The number *seven* plays a significant role. According to Hebrew tradition, this number spoke of *completeness*. There are Seven Messages to the Seven Churches (2:1—3:22), which are mentioned by name. There are Seven Seals (6:1–17), Seven Trumpets (8:6—11:19), Seven Personages (12:1—14:20), Seven Vials (bowls) of God's Wrath (16:1–21), and Seven Final Judgments (17:1—20:15). Finally, there are Seven Wonderful Blessings (21:1—22:5).

In like manner, *thousand* also means perfection or completeness (cp. Psalm 90:4). The Church is pictured as being complete, reflected in twelve thousand being saved from each of the twelve tribes of [spiritual?] Israel (7:1–8). And Satan is bound for a thousand years that "he should deceive the nations no more" (20:3). In a negative sense, the number 3 ½ is associated with Satan (11:2; 13:5). We read of a 42 month (or 3 ½ years) period. This number is designed to symbolize a diminishing of the visible glory and power of God on earth.

The Content and Place of the *Revelation*

Like its counterparts, the *Book of the Revelation* depicts the end of the present age and the coming of God's future kingdom through symbols, images, and numbers. These symbols include an angel whose legs are pillars of fire, men who ride on horses while smiting the earth with plagues of destruction, and a fiery red dragon with seven heads and ten horns, who crouches before a heavenly woman about to deliver a child.

Why was apocalyptic literature written in such imagery? One reason is that these books were written in dangerous times—when it was safer to hide one's message in images than to speak plainly. Moreover, the symbolism preserved an element of mystery about details of time and place. The purpose of such symbolism, however, was not to confuse, but to inform and strengthen believers in the face of persecution. Although the keys to some symbols have been lost, the overall message of this book is clear: God is all-powerful. No countermoves of the devil, no matter how strong, can frustrate the righteous purposes of God.

John tells us, "The seven heads [of the beast] are seven mountains" (17:9), which may be identified as the famed seven hills of Rome (Chapter 13). The cryptic words tell us that the dragon (Satan) gave authority to the beast (Rome) to exact worship from its inhabitants (13:4).

The Structure of the Book

The *Book of the Revelation* contains seven visions interspersed with six "interludes." The visions focus on activity upon the earth, while most of the interludes observe activity in heaven.

The First Vision (chaps. 1–3) is of the resurrected Christ challenging His Church to remain loyal in the midst of great tribulation.

The Second Vision (chaps. 4–7) is of Christ the Slain Lamb standing with a sealed scroll before God the Father in heaven. As the Lamb opens each of the seven seals containing the destinies of individuals and nations, a series of disasters befalls the earth.

A series of seven angels blowing seven trumpets forms *the Third Vision* (chaps. 8–11). At the sound of these trumpets, divine judgment falls again.

The Fourth Vision (chaps. 12–14) consists of the persecution by Satan and the Beast of the Church.

The Fifth Vision (chaps. 15–16) contains another series of seven: seven bowls pouring out God's wrath.

The Sixth Vision brings into focus the judgment of Babylon (a symbol for Rome) (chaps. 17:1—19:10).

The Seventh Vision promises a final victory, final judgment, and final blessedness (chap. 19:11–22). There will be a glorious future for the people of God. Christ has promised to make all things new: a new heaven, a new earth, and a new Jerusalem (21). And because of this, the heart of the Christian cries out, "Come, Lord Jesus!" (22:20).

The Seven Churches of the *Revelation*

Ephesus (2:1) refers to a city in Lydia in western Asia Minor. It was located on an important trade route and was the capital of the province of Asia when Rome ruled the world. The city was devoted to the goddess Diana. Paul visited the city (Acts 18:19ff; 19:8ff) and then remained for two years (Acts 19:8, 10) to establish a church.

Smyrna (2:8) refers to an ancient city on the western coast of Asia Minor. It was occupied by the Aeolian Greeks, and later by the Ionian Greeks. It was destroyed by Alyattes of Lydia (580 B.C.) but rebuilt by Alexander the Great. It became a leading commercial center, and later became part of the Roman province of Asia.

Pergamum (2:12) was a very important city in ancient Mysia in western Asia Minor, 15 miles from the Aegean Sea. The "seat of Satan" that is mentioned may refer to the great altar of Zeus which overlooked the town. Pergamum was the base for the official cult of emperor worship. The Temple of Asclepius was considered to be a source of healing power.

Thyatira (2:18) refers to a city of Lydia, Asia Minor. It was on the road from Pergamum to Sardis. The residents of Thyatira were famous for their skills in dyeing (Acts 16:14). John wrote a letter to the church of Thyatira.

Sardis (3:1) refers to a city in western Asia Minor at the foot of Mount Tmolus on the east bank of the Hermus River, 50 miles east of Smyrna. It was the capital of Croesus. Sardis was conquered (546 B.C.) by Cyrus of Persia and then later by Alexander, Antiochus, and the Romans—who made it part of the province of Asia.

Philadelphia (3:7) refers to a city of Lydia, in western Asia Minor, about 28 miles southeast of Sardis.

Laodicea (3:14) refers to a city in Asia Minor near Colossae. It was named for Laodice, wife of Antiochus II (261–246 B.C.). At Laodicea, a church of Jesus Christ was established (Col. 2:1, 4:16). The people were wealthy but spiritually poor. Laodicea provided a famous eye salve—but the people needed a spiritual eye salve (Rev. 3:18).

Problems in the Seven Churches

Ephesus	left their first love
Smyrna	(none mentioned)
Pergamum	licentiousness (living for self-pleasure, *vs.* holiness)
Thyatira	tolerance of immorality
Sardis	spiritual deadness
Philadelphia	(none mentioned)
Laodicea	lukewarm

Promises to the Seven Churches

Ephesus	eat of the Tree of Life	2:7 cp. 22:2
Smyrna	escape the Second Death	2:11 cp. 20:6; 21:3, 7, 8
Pergamos	receive a new name	2:17 cp. 21:27; 20:15; 22:4
Thyatira	have authority over nations	2:26–28 cp. 21:24–26; 22:1–3
Sardis	remain in the Book of Life	3:5 cp. 19:8

| Philadelphia | be part of the New Jerusalem | 3:12 cp. 21:10; 22:4 |
| Laodicea | sit with Christ | 3:21 cp. 21:3, 5; 22:1–3 |

The Millennium (20:1–10)[2]

The thousand-year period of Christ's rule described in 20:1–10 is commonly called *The Millennium*, and is understood in various ways.

Premillennialists believe that the thousand years follow the Second Coming that is described in 19:11–21. After the Second Coming, Satan is bound and Christ ushers in a long period of earthly peace and prosperity. Some think of this as a literal thousand years, while others consider the number to mean a very long period of time. Christians receive resurrection bodies at the beginning of The Millennium, but the final judgment for all others takes place at the end, after a rebellion led by Satan. In the second century, Justin Martyr and Papias were among those holding a premillennial view.

Amillennialists understand The Millennium to be a picture of the present reign of Christ ("the kingdom of God is within you," Luke 17:21) and of the saints in heaven (analogous to 6:9–10). The "first resurrection" (20:5) is either the life of Christians who have died and are with Christ in heaven, or life in Christ that starts with spiritual new birth (Rom. 6:8–11, Eph. 2:6, Col. 3:1–4). Satan has been bound through the triumph of Christ in His crucifixion and resurrection (John 12:31, Col. 2:15).

Postmillennialists believe that the kingdom of Christ and the Church will experience much more expansion on earth before the Second Coming. The thousand years are understood by some as a final period of earthly Christian triumph following the spread of the gospel. Others agree with amillennialists in identifying 20:1–6 with the entire period that begins with the resurrection of Christ.

---

[2] This section is abstracted from *The New Geneva Study Bible*, published 1995 by Thomas Nelson Publishers, pages 2004–05.

The different understandings partly concern the chronological relation of 20:1–6 to 19:11–21. Premillennialists believe that the events described in 20:1–10 simply follow the Second Coming, which is depicted in 19:11–21. But 20:1–15 might also represent a seventh cycle of judgments leading up to the Second Coming. The final battle in 20:7–10 seems to be the same as the final battle in 16:14, 16; 17:14; 19:11–21. Similar language from Ezekiel 8—39 is used in the various descriptions. The judgment of Satan in 20:10 parallels the judgments against Babylon (ch. 17–18) and against the Beast and the False Prophet (19:11—20:10). These enemies of God are consigned to everlasting punishment, and the visions depicting their judgment may be parallel descriptions rather than different events in a sequence. Certain features in 20:11–15 correspond to earlier descriptions of the Second Coming (6:14, 11:18). Most important, all of Christ's enemies have been judged in 19:11–21. If 20:1–6 represents later events, there would be no one left for Satan to deceive in 20:3.

Caution is needed because the different millennial positions depend on the interpretation of Old Testament prophetic texts as well as these verses in the *Revelation*. Moreover, like most of the *Revelation*, 20:1–10 uses language that in principle may legitimately be capable of multiple fulfillments. These facts make precise interpretation difficult. It is God's prerogative to reveal only as much about the order of future events as is good for us to know (cp. Acts 1:7).

The *Revelation:* An Expanded Outline

Lord of the Church (1—3)

I. The Prologue: A Preview of Coming Glory	1:1–8
II. The Command to Communicate	1:9–20
III. Seven Messages to the Seven Churches	
A. Ephesus	2:1–7

B. Smyrna	2:8–11
C. Pergamum	2:12–17
D. Thyatira	2:18–29
E. Sardis	3:1–6
F. Philadelphia	3:7–13
G. Laodicea	3:14–22

Lord of the Earth (4—20)

IV. The Vision Unfolds from the Very Throne of God

A. A doorway to heavenly delights		4:1
B. The throne of God		4:2–3, 5–6
C. Twenty-four Elders and Four Beasts		4:4–8
1. First Beast	like a lion	4:7
2. Second Beast	like a calf	4:7
3. Third Beast	like a man	4:7
4. Fourth Beast	like a flying eagle	4:7
D. The scroll (book) sealed with seven seals		5:1–14
1. The scroll in the right hand [of power]		5:1
2. Search for one worthy to open the scroll		5:2–5
3. Worthy is the Lamb		5:6–7
4. The rejoicing of the righteous ones		5:8–14
E. The breaking of the Seven Seals		6:1—8:5
1. The First Seal	a rider on a white horse	6:1–3
2. The Second Seal	a rider on a red horse	6:4
3. The Third Seal	a rider on a black horse	6:4
4. The Fourth Seal	a rider on a pale horse	6:7–8
5. The Fifth Seal	the souls of the saints	6:9–11
6. The Sixth Seal	changes in the universe	6:12–17

First Interlude   7:1–17

Before the opening of the Seventh Seal, there was the first of Six Interludes. John is a witness to the sealing of the 144,000 Jews (7:1–8) and a great multitude of Gentiles washed by the blood of the Lamb (7:9–17).

    7. The Seventh Seal was broken   8:1
       Then there was silence in heaven for the space of half an hour. Divine preparations were made by seven angels which stood before God. They were given Seven Trumpets. Another angel was given a golden censer to offer incense, with the prayers of the saints (8:3–5) offered upon the golden altar which was before the throne.

  F. The sounding of the seven trumpets   8:6—11:19
    1. First Trumpet   hail, fire, and blood   8:6–7
    2. Second Trumpet   pollution of the seas   8:8–9
    3. Third Trumpet   pollution of the rivers   8:10–11
    4. Fourth Trumpet   sun/moon/stars affected 8:12–13
    5. Fifth Trumpet   killing of men
      a. First Woe   plague of locusts   9:12
    6. The Sixth Trumpet great slaughter
      b. Second Woe   an army of horsemen   9:13–21
      c. Third Woe   fire, smoke, brimstone

Second Interlude   10:1—11:14

During this second interlude, John bears witness to a little scroll (10:1–11) and saw two witnesses (11:1–14). Attention was paid to these witnesses:

      - their association with the temple   11:1–2
      - the duration of their ministry   11:3
      - their personal protection and power   11:4–6
      - the termination of their ministry   11:7–10
      - their ultimate translation.   11:11–14

7. The Seventh Trumpet sounded to announce the sovereign reign of the Lord over the nations of the earth (11:15–19). The nations resisted the reign of the Sovereign with violence.

  G. Seven Personages   12:1–14:20

1. First Person	woman clothed with sun	12:1–2
2. Second Person	a great red dragon	12:3–4
3. Third Person	a man child	12:5–6
4. Fourth Person	the archangel	12:7–12
5. Fifth Person	the woman with child	12:13–17
6. Sixth Person	the beast out of the sea	13:1–10
7. Seventh Person	the beast out of the earth	13:11–18

Third Interlude   14:1–20

After the description of the seven personages, John heard various announcements proclaimed concerning:

- The Lamb on Mount Zion and the 144,000	*14:1–5*
- The proclamation of the everlasting gospel	*14:6–8*
- The worship of the beast	*14:9–13*
- The blessed dead and a great harvest.	*14:14–20*

  H. The prelude to the seven bowl judgments began as John saw a sea of glass (15:2–4). Angels came out of the temple of the tabernacle of the testimony in heaven (15:5–8).

1. First Bowl	boils	16:1–2
2. Second Bowl	blood in the seas	16:3
3. Third Bowl	blood in the water	16:4–7
4. Fourth Bowl	scorching heat	16:8–9
5. Fifth Bowl	darkness	16:10–11
6. Sixth Bowl	Euphrates River dried up	16:12–16

Fourth Interlude: Prelude to Armageddon

During this fourth interlude, John observed three unclean spirits coming out of the mouths of the dragon, the beast, and the false prophet (16:13–16).

    7. Seventh Bowl   great hail   16:17–21

I. The vision of John entered into a final phase as he witnessed the seven final judgments (17:1) which we call *Armageddon*.
    1. First Judgment   religious Babylon   17:1–18
    2. Second Judgment   commercial Babylon   18:1–24
    An appeal is made to the people:
    - to be separate from the corrupt system   18:4–8
    - because suffering will be certain   18:9–10
    - just judgment caused joy for the elect.   18:20–24

Fifth Interlude   19:1–21

During a fifth interlude the apostle anticipates the coming of Christ:
    - there is a hallelujah chorus   19:1–7
    - followed by a marriage supper   19:8–10
    - and defeat of all enemies of the Lord.   19:11–21

    3. Third Judgment   False Prophet & Beast   19:20
    4. Fourth Judgment   the nations   19:21

Sixth Interlude

In this interlude John observes:
    - The binding of Satan   20:1–3
    - The blessed first resurrection   20:4–6
    - A burst of rebellion.   20:7–9

    5. Fifth Judgment   on Gog and Magog   20:8–9

| 6. Sixth Judgment | on Satan | 20:10 |
| 7. Seventh Judgment | on the wicked dead | 20:11–15 |

Lord of the New Heaven and New Earth (21—22)

Seven wonderful blessings, together with the crucifixion and resurrection of Jesus Christ, form the climax of the Bible as eternity future is unveiled:

1. A new heaven	21:1
2. A new earth	21:2–8
3. A new city	21:9–23
4. A new order of nations	21:24–27
5. A river of life	22:1
6. A tree of life	22:2
7. An eternal throne.	22:3–5

Conclusion

The Apostle John closes the *Book of the Revelation* with:

- words of comfort	22:6–17
- words of warning	22:18–19
- words of blessing.	22:20–21

> *"He which testifieth these things saith,*
> *'Surely I come quickly.' Amen.*
> *Even so, come, Lord Jesus.*
> *The grace of our*
> *Lord Jesus Christ*
> *be with you all. Amen."*
>
> —REVELATION 22:20–21

Appendix 1

35 Miracles of the Master

"Say ye . . . 'Thou blasphemest;' because I said, 'I am the Son of God?' If I do not the works of My Father, believe Me not. But if I do, though ye believe not Me, believe the works [miracles]: that ye may know, and believe, that the Father is in Me, and I in Him."

—John 10:36–38

1. The changing of water into wine — John 2:7–9
2. The healing of the nobleman's son — John 4:50
3. The healing of the demoniac — Mark 1:25; Luke 4:35
4. The healing of Peter's mother-in-law — Mark 1:31; Luke 4:39
5. The catching of many fish — Luke 5:5
6. The healing of a leper — Matt. 8:3; Mark 1:41
7. The healing of a paralytic — Matt. 9:2, 6–7; Mk. 2:5, 10–12
8. The healing of a withered hand — Matt. 12:13; Mark 3:5
9. The healing of a centurion's son — Matt. 8:13; Luke 7:10
10. The resurrection of a widow's son — Luke 7:14
11. The calming of the storm at sea — Matt. 8:26; Mark 4:39
12. The healing of the Gadarene demoniac — Matt. 8:32; Mark 5:8
13. The healing of a bleeding woman — Matt. 9:22; Mark 5:29
14. The resurrection of Jarius' daughter — Matt. 9:25; Mark 5:41
15. The healing of two blind men — Matt. 9:29
16. The healing of a demoniac — Matt. 9:33

17. The healing of an invalid	John 5:8
18. The feeding of the 5,000	Matt. 14:19; Mark 6:41
19. Walking on the waves	Matt. 14:25; Mark 6:48
20. The healing of a demoniac girl	Matt. 15:28; Mark 7:29
21. The healing of a deaf man	Mark 7:34–35
22. The feeding of the 4,000	Matt. 15:35; Mark 8:6
23. The healing of a blind man	Mark 8:25
24. The healing of a man born blind	John 9:7
25. The healing of a demoniac boy	Matt. 17:18; Mark 9:25
26. The catching of an unusual fish	Matt. 17:27
27. The healing of a blind demoniac	Matt. 12:22; Luke 11:14
28. The healing of a woman in bondage	Luke 13:10–17
29. The healing of a man with dropsy	Luke 14:4
30. The healing of ten lepers	Luke 17:11–19
31. The resurrection of Lazarus	John 11:43–44
32. The healing of two blind men	Matt. 20:34; Luke 18:42
33. The cursing of a fig tree	Matt. 21:19; Mark 11:14
34. The curing of a severed ear	Matt. 26:51; Mark 14:47
35. The catching of many fish	John 21:6

Appendix 2

Guidelines for Reading the Bible

(Suggested by Dr. William Smith, *Dictionary of the Bible*)

1. Consider the times, places, and circumstances of the sacred writers.
2. Become familiar with the geography of Scripture.
3. Discern as far as possible the normal, literal, and primary meaning.
4. Beware of mystical interpretation; not every passage is spiritualized.
5. Seek the literal before the spiritualized meaning.
6. The true spiritual sense of a passage is to be highly valued.
7. Avoid novel interpretations.
8. Allow for idiomatic and figurative expressions, especially when an absurdity would follow from departing from the literal sense.
9. Distinguish between plain and figurative language.
10. Do not carry a metaphor too far.
11. Consider the whole context of a passage before any conclusion is drawn from a single verse.
12. Consider as best as possible to whom a passage is written, by whom it was written, and for what purpose it was written.
13. Compare spiritual things with spiritual by comparing Scripture with Scripture. Let the New Testament interpret the Old Testament and when it does, accept that interpretation without seeking another.
14. Explain what is difficult by what is plain and easy to understand.

15. Never expect to fully understand all that is in the Scriptures. A wise, humble, devout, and consistent study of the Scriptures will add to personal understanding.
16. When words and phrases are obscure and difficult to understand, do not force an interpretation and pretend to have understanding.
17. Realize that a word can have different meanings in different passages.
18. Learn the great concepts behind the important words of the Bible: faith, repentance, redemption, justification, sanctification, grace, and righteousness.
19. Consider the personality of the author, the condition and character to whom he writes, the errors which are opposed, and the truths which are established.
20. The New Testament is the fulfillment of the Old. Carefully compare them with each other.
21. Be aware of the fact that the historical and prophetic books of the Old Testament illustrate each other.
22. Be aware of the fact that the *Epistles* of the New Testament are a Divine commentary on the four *Gospels*.
23. *Hebrews* is the Divine commentary on the Jewish rituals.
24. Read the whole book that is to be studied in one sitting prior to any formal study.
25. Do not form an opinion from a small part of a passage.
26. Be content to remain without clear understanding rather than accept error over a difficult passage.
27. Remember that no doctrine will disagree with something that is taught in another portion of Scripture.
28. Interpret all that is said of the Lord God in a way that is consistent with infinite perfections.
29. Do not force types and allegories on any portion of Scripture.
30. Do not force a parable to bear a spiritual meaning it does not teach. Do not force a parable to bear a literal meaning it does not teach.

31. Remember that the whole of a truth is sometimes put for a part, and a part is sometimes put for the whole.
32. Remember that general terms are sometimes limited, particular terms are sometimes used for general, and definite numbers are often put for indefinite numbers.
33. Remember that sometimes things represented by the hyperbole are magnified or diminished beyond or below their limits.
34. Remember that negatives are often used for a strong affirmation of the contrary, such as "not guiltless," for "exceedingly guilty" and "shall not be moved" for "shall be firmly established."
35. Remember that questions are often used for strong affirmations or negations (Jer. 5:9; Mark 8:36).
36. Read the poetic books by the nature of the Hebrew verse.
37. Do not interpret prophecy or history by speculation or conjecture.
38. Remember that the sacred writers often changed persons and tenses.
39. Remember that some truths are set forth in the form of absolute and universal statements that are to be interpreted under certain limitations and conditions. For example, "all" does not always mean "all without exception" (cp. Luke 2:3).
40. Remember that one principle or duty is often used to teach an universal gospel duty (as found in Ephesians 5:18).
41. Promises made to particular persons in Scripture may be applied to all true believers.
42. Never separate gospel duties from holy promises nor gospel promises from holy duties.
43. Remember that whatever we read in the Bible is to be read as God's Word to us as individuals.